Help Me! Guide to the iPad Pro

By Charles Hughes

This guide covers the 12.9-inch iPad Pro, released on November 11, 2015, and the 9.7-inch iPad Pro, released on March 31, 2016.

Table of Contents

Getting Started

Table of Contents

1. Button Layout

The iPad has four buttons. The rest of the functionality is controlled by the touchscreen. Each button has several functions, depending on the context in which it is used.

The buttons perform the following functions:

Figure 1: Top View

Sleep/Wake Button

- Turns the iPad on and off.
- Locks and unlocks the iPad.

Headphone Jack - Allows headphones or speakers to be plugged in. Allows an AUX cable to be plugged in to hear the iPad over the speakers in a car or stereo.

Home Button

Figure 2: Front View

Home Button

- Shows the Home screen.
- Displays open applications when pressed twice quickly.

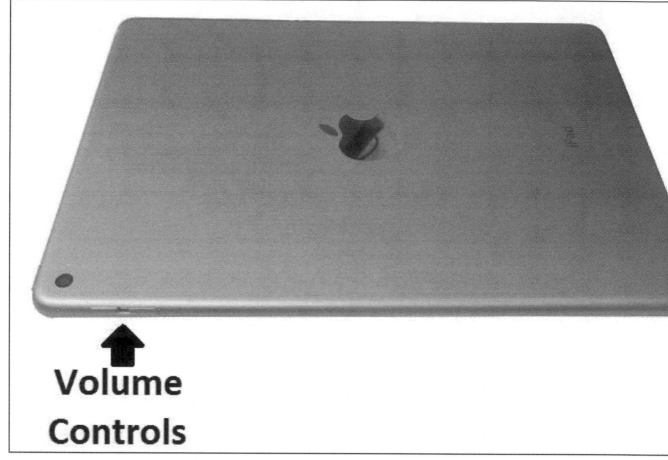

Volume Controls

Figure 3: Right Side View

Volume Controls

- Controls the volume of the ringer. Refer to *"Adjusting Sound Settings"* on page 218 to learn more about setting ringtones or setting the sound volume.
- Controls the media volume.

Lightning Connector

Figure 4: Bottom View

Lightning Connector - Connects the iPad to a computer in order to transfer data. Connects the iPad to a charger.

2. Charging the iPad

To ensure that the iPad works well, please follow these guidelines:

Note: You cannot use a cable that came with an iPad 3 (March 2012) or earlier to charge an iPad Pro.

Discharge the iPad completely at least once a month for optimal performance. When charging the battery, the meter in the upper right-hand corner of the screen (when unlocked) may show that it is fully charged; however, the charge is not complete until **100% Charged** appears on the lock screen. Insert the Lightning cable into the Lightning Connector on the bottom of the iPad. The

lightning cable looks like this: . When the cable is inserted correctly, the indicator sound is played. There is no incorrect way to insert a lightning cable, as long as it fits into the lightning connector without the use of force. Refer to *"Tips and Tricks"* on page 301 to learn about conserving battery life.

3. Turning the iPad On and Off

Use the Sleep/Wake button to turn the iPad on or off. To turn the iPad on, press and hold the **Sleep/Wake** button for two seconds. The iPad turns on and the logo is displayed. After the iPad has finished starting up, the Lock screen is displayed.

Note: If the iPad does not turn on after a few seconds, try charging the battery.

To turn the iPad off, press and hold the **Sleep/Wake** button until the screen becomes dark. The message "Slide to power off" appears. Touch the slider and move your finger to the right. The iPad turns off.

*Note: To keep the iPad on, touch **Cancel** or do not take any action at all.*

4. Installing a SIM Card (iPad 4G models only)

Insert the SIM card from an old iPhone or iPad to retain your personal information and phone number. The type of SIM card that you need depends on your carrier. For instance, you cannot insert a Verizon SIM card into an AT&T iPad, and vice-versa. To install a SIM card:

1. Insert the end of a paper clip or a SIM eject tool into the small hole on the right side of the iPad. The SIM card tray pops out.
2. Take out the old SIM card, if necessary, and insert the new SIM card with the short side facing upwards.

3. Re-insert the tray into the iPad. The new SIM card is installed.

5. Setting Up the iPad for the First Time

You must set up the iPad when you turn it on for the first time, unless an Apple associate or another specialist has already done so for you. To set up the iPad:

1. Turn on the iPad by pressing and holding the **Sleep/Wake** button until the icon appears. The iPad starts up and the Welcome screen appears.
2. Touch the screen anywhere and move your finger to the right to begin setting up your iPad. The Language screen appears.
3. Touch a language in the list. The language is selected, and the Country screen appears.
4. Touch the country where you reside. The country is selected, and the Wi-Fi Networks screen appears.
5. Touch a Wi-Fi network. The Password prompt appears.
6. Enter the network password, which is usually found on your wireless router. Touch **Join**. The iPad connects to the selected Wi-Fi network and the Location Services screen appears. If you did not activate your iPad in the store, you may need to confirm your phone number before the Location Services screen appears. Enter your billing zip code and the last four digits of your social security number to confirm.
7. Touch **Enable Location Services** if you want to turn the feature on. Touch **Disable Location Services** to leave the feature turned off. Some applications do not work with Location Services turned off. The Set Up iPad screen appears.
8. Touch **Restore from iCloud Backup** or **Restore from iTunes Backup** if you have a data backup. You need to connect the iPad to your computer and run iTunes if you touch 'Restore from iTunes Backup'. Touch **Set Up as New iPad** if you do not have an iCloud or iTunes backup. The Apple ID screen appears.
9. Touch **Sign In with your Apple ID** if you have an Apple ID, or touch **Create a Free Apple ID** to set up a new one. The Terms and Conditions screen appears once you are signed in.
10. Touch **Agree** in the bottom right-hand corner of the screen. A confirmation dialog appears.
11. Touch **Agree** again. The iCloud screen appears.
12. Touch **Use iCloud** to use the feature or touch **Don't Use iCloud** to disable it. The Find My iPad feature (iPhone or iPad) is turned on automatically when you use iCloud. The iMessage and FaceTime screen appears.
13. Touch a phone number or email address if you would like to enable it for iMessage or FaceTime. A blue check mark appears next to each selected address or number.

14. Touch **Next** in the upper right-hand corner of the screen when you are finished. The iCloud drive screen appears. iCloud Drive syncs all of your documents and images in iCloud, and updates them on all of your iPads as you work.

15. Touch **Upgrade to iCloud Drive**. iCloud Drive is turned on, and the Passcode Creation screen appears.

16. Enter a passcode to set up a security lock for your phone, or touch **Don't Add Passcode** to do it later. The Diagnostics screen appears.

17. Touch **Automatically Send** to have the iPad send usage data to Apple or touch **Don't Send** to disable this feature. Usage Data contains anonymous statistics about the ways in which you use your iPad.

18. Touch **Get Started**. The iPad setup is complete.

6. Navigating the Screens

There are many ways to navigate the iPad. You can perform the following actions using your finger or the Apple Pencil. Use the following tips to quickly navigate the screens of the iPad:

- Use the **Home** button to return to the Home screen at any time. Any application that you were using is in the same state when you return to it.

- At the Home screen, slide your finger to the left to access additional pages. If nothing happens, the other pages are blank.

- Touch the center of the Home screen and slide your finger down to access the iPad's search feature. You may search any data stored on your phone, including application data, as well as the web, iTunes, Application Store, movie show times, locations nearby, and much more.

7. Organizing Icons

You may wish to re-order the location of the application icons on the screens. To organize application icons:

1. Touch an icon, and hold it until all of the icons begin to shake. The icons can now be moved around the screen.
2. Move the icon to the desired location and let go of the screen. The icon is relocated and the surrounding icons are re-ordered accordingly. If an icon that used to be on the screen is gone, then it has been moved to a different Home screen in the process.

3. To move an icon to another screen, move the icon to the edge of the current one and hold it there. The adjacent screen appears. Drop the icon in the desired location.
4. Press the **Home** button. The icons stop shaking.

8. Creating an Icon Folder

When there are many icons on the Home screens, you may wish to organize the icons into folders. Each folder can have a meaningful name to enable you to find the icons easily. To create a folder:

1. Touch an icon and hold it until all of the icons begin to shake. The icons can now be moved.
2. Move one icon on top of another and let go of the screen. A folder with the selected icons is created, as shown in **Figure 5**. Touch the ⊗ button to enter a name for the folder.
3. Enter a name for the folder, and touch **Done**. The new name is saved.
4. To exit the folder, touch anywhere outside of it. The folder closes.
5. Press the **Home** button. The icons stop shaking.

Note: To add more icons to a folder, just touch an icon while it is shaking and move it onto the folder.

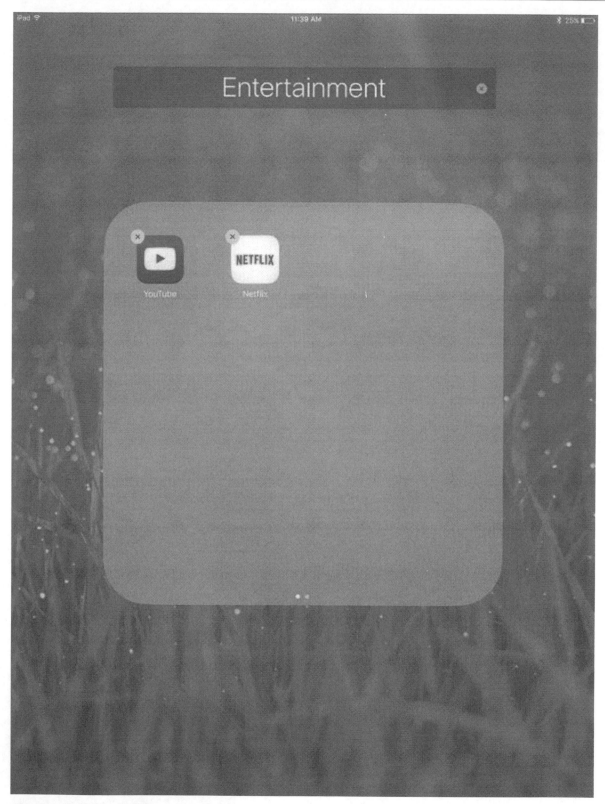

Figure 5: New Folder

9. Using Wi-Fi

Use a nearby Wi-Fi hotspot or a home router to avoid having to use data. Wi-Fi is required to download large applications. To turn on Wi-Fi:

1. Touch the icon. The Settings screen appears, as shown in **Figure 6**.
2. Touch **Wi-Fi**. The Wi-Fi Networks screen appears, as shown in **Figure 7**.
3. Touch the switch next to 'Wi-Fi'. Wi-Fi turns on and a list of available networks appears, as shown in **Figure 8**. If the network has an icon next to it, a password is needed to connect to it.
4. Touch the network to which you would like to connect. The Wi-Fi Password prompt appears if the network is protected, as shown in **Figure 9**.
5. Enter the network password. Touch **Join**. Provided that you entered the correct password, a check mark appears next to the network name and the icon appears at the top of the screen. You are connected to the Wi-Fi network.

Note: If you enter an incorrect password, the message "Unable to join the network >Network Name<" appears, where '>Network Name<' is the name of your network. The network password is usually written on the modem given to you by your internet service provider. It is sometimes called a WEP Key.

Figure 6: Settings Screen

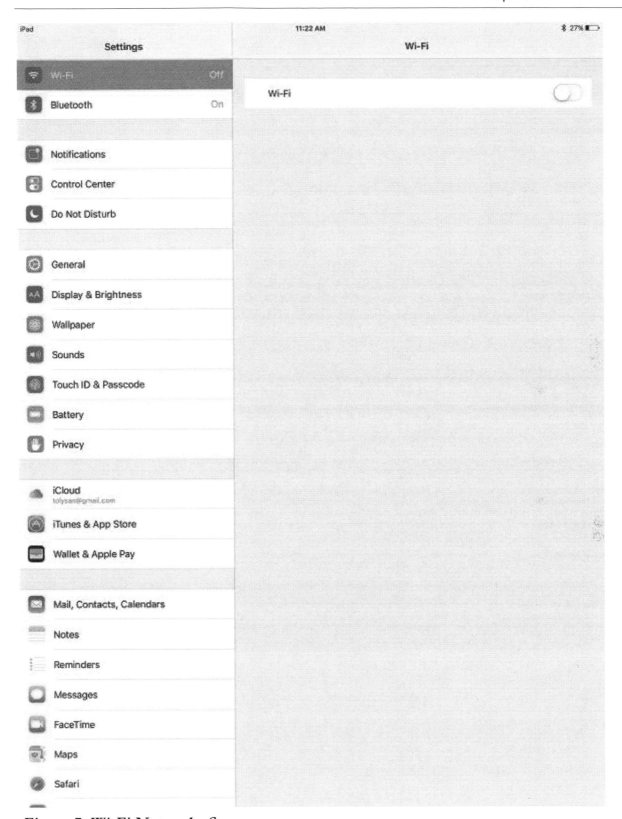

Figure 7: Wi-Fi Networks Screen

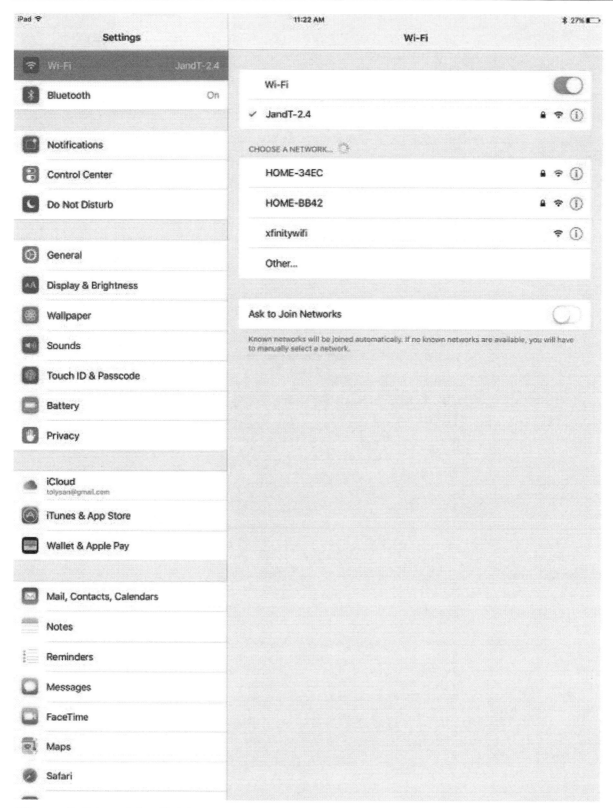

Figure 8: List of Available Wi-Fi Networks

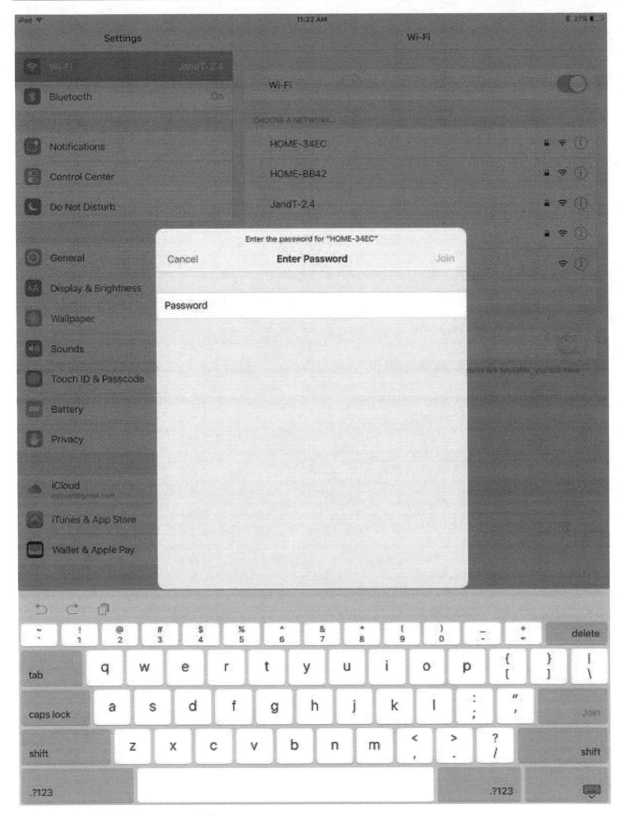

Figure 9: Wi-Fi Password Prompt

10. Accessing Quick Settings through the Control Center

There are various settings that you can access without opening the Settings screen by using the Control Center. To use the Control Center:

1. Touch the bottom of the screen at any time and slide your finger up. The Control Center appears, as shown in **Figure 10**.
2. Touch one of the following icons at the top of the Control Center to turn on the corresponding function:

 - Turns Airplane mode on or off.

 - Turns Wi-Fi on or off.

 - Turns Bluetooth on or off.

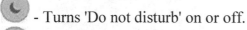 - Turns 'Do not disturb' on or off.

 - Turns automatic screen rotation on or off.

 - Mutes all sounds on the iPad.

A white icon, such as a [icon] icon, indicates that the function is turned on.

3. Touch one of the following icons at the bottom of the Control Center to turn on the corresponding service:

[icon] - Opens the timer application.

[icon] - Turns on the camera.

[icon] - Turns on Night Shift mode, which softens the colors to make the screen easier on the eyes.

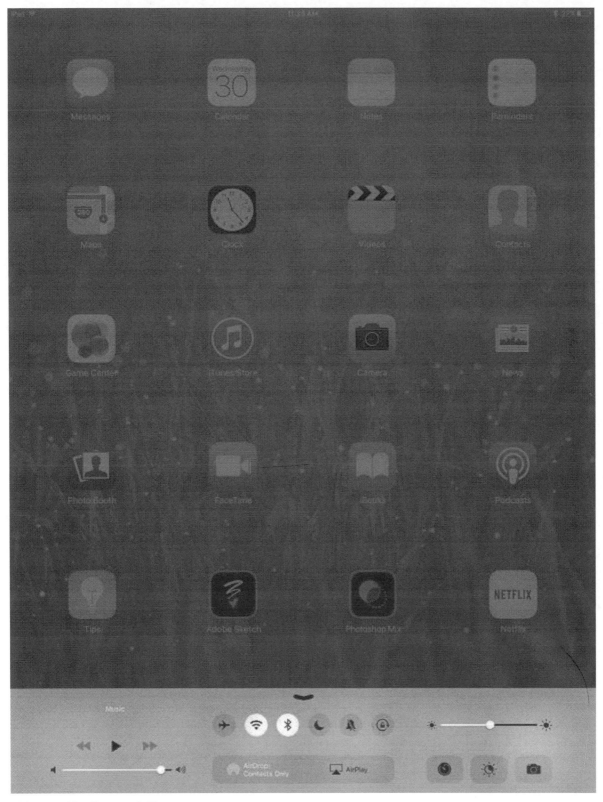

Figure 10: Control Center

11. Using the Notification Center

The Notification Center shows event reminders, alerts, such as calendar events, received messages, missed calls, and widgets. To open the notification center, touch the top of the screen at any time and move your finger down. Use the following tips when working in the Notification Center:

- Touch a notification to open the corresponding application. For instance, touch a calendar event to open the calendar.

- Touch **All** or **Missed** at the top of the screen to view the corresponding call notifications.

- Touch **Widgets** to view reminders and the battery charge of the iPad and Apple Pencil.

Using the Apple Pencil

Table of Contents

1. What the Apple Pencil Can and Cannot Do

The Apple Pencil is Apple's first-generation stylus, which only works with the iPad Pro 12.9 and 9.7. The Apple Pencil has many features, but also comes with several limitations. Any limitation listed below indicates that you must use your finger to perform the action.

Apple Pencil Features

- Draw and take notes, even when tracing through paper
- Open applications and links
- Scroll through webpages, lists, messages, and menus
- Type on the keyboard, enter lockscreen passwords, and bring up the search (slide down from the center of the Home screen)
- Unlock the iPad
- Lay your hand on the the iPad without interfering with what you're writing or drawing (Palm Rejection)
- Charge using the Lightning Port on your iPad or the included adapter, which lets you charge the
- Pencil using a standard lightning cable

Apple Pencil Limitations

- Cannot open the Notification or Control centers

- Cannot use Slide Over or Split View multitasking tools

- Cannot use the dull end of the Pencil as an eraser

- Cannot use multi-finger gestures

- Cannot use the Pencil with any device other than the iPad Pro

2. Connecting the Apple Pencil to the iPad Pro

Before you can use the Apple Pencil with the iPad Pro, pair it with the iPad. To pair the Pencil, make sure that Bluetooth is turned on. Refer to *"Turning Bluetooth On or Off"* on page 214 to learn how. To connect the Pencil:

1. Once Bluetooth is turned on, open the cap on top of the Pencil to expose the connector. Connect the Pencil to the lightning port on the iPad. Refer to *"Button Layout"* on page 9 to learn how to find the lightning port.
2. The Bluetooth Pairing Request appears, as shown in **Figure 1**.
3. Touch **Pair**. The Apple Pencil is now connected and ready for use. Disconnect the Pencil from the Lightning Port and use it as a stylus.

Note: If you turn off Bluetooth, the Apple Pencil will disconnect. You will need to turn on Bluetooth and plug the Pencil in to the Lightning Port again to reconnect it. Once it is unplugged, it is once again ready for use.

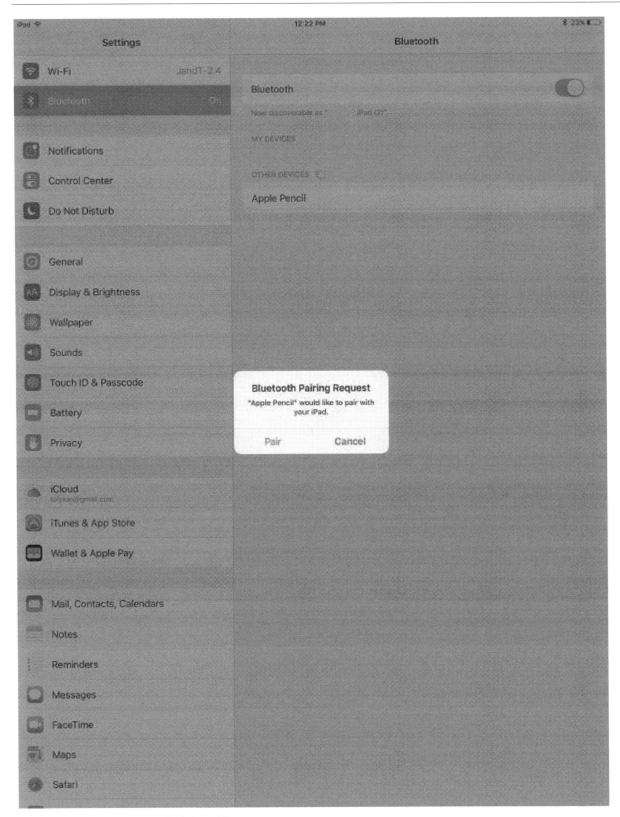

Figure 1: Bluetooth Pairing Request

3. Charging the Apple Pencil

To charge the Apple Pencil, remove the cap from the top and plug it in to your iPad Pro. You can also use the adapter included with the Apple Pencil to charge it using your iPad charger.

4. Using the Apple Pencil to Take Notes

To take notes using the Apple Pencil, use the Notes application that comes pre-installed on the iPad Pro, or download another application, such as Notability. In the Notes application, touch

the icon to take notes using the Pencil. While taking notes, you can place your hand down on the screen without affecting the note. You can also lay a piece of paper on the iPad and draw through it, which is useful when you want to use another drawing as a stencil and transfer it to the iPad.

5. Sketching with the Apple Pencil

The Apple Pencil also allows you to draw, which can be done in the Notes application, or in another application such as Adobe Sketch. Use the following tips when sketching with the Apple Pencil:

- Apply more pressure to the screen to increase the width of the line.
- Angle the Pencil to draw thick lines when shading.

6. Replacing the Tip

The Apple Pencil comes with a replacement tip, in case you break or lose yours. To replace the tip, unscrew the tip counter-clockwise, and screw on the new one.

Managing Contacts

Table of Contents

1. Adding a New Contact

The iPad can store phone numbers, email addresses, and other Contact Information in the phonebook. To add a new contact to the phonebook:

Note: For some unexplained reason, Apple has decided to place the Contacts icon in the Extras folder by default. If you cannot find it, look in that folder.

1. Touch the icon on the Home screen. The phonebook appears.
2. Touch the button at the top of the screen. The New Contact screen appears, as shown in **Figure 1**.
3. Touch **First**. The keyboard appears. Enter the first name of the contact.
4. Touch **Last**. Enter the last name of the contact.
5. Touch any empty field to enter the desired information, and then touch **Done** in the upper right-hand corner of the screen. The contact's information is stored.

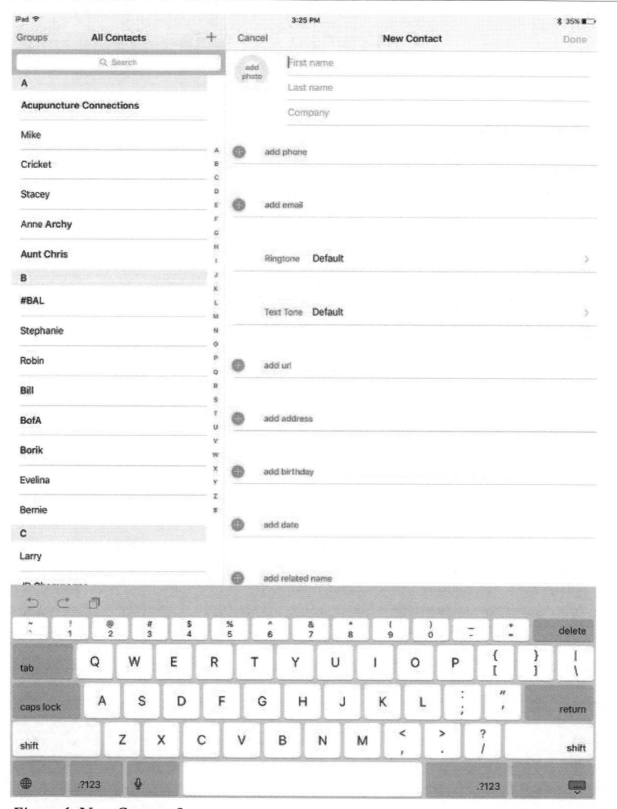

Figure 1: New Contact Screen

2. Finding a Contact

After adding contacts to your iPad's phonebook, you may search for them. To find a stored contact:

1. Touch the ![icon] icon on the Home screen. The phonebook appears.
2. Touch **Search** at the top of the screen. The keyboard appears.
3. Start typing the name of a contact. Contact matches appear as you type, as shown in **Figure 2**.
4. Touch a match. The Contact Info screen appears, as shown in **Figure 3**.

Figure 2: Contact Matches

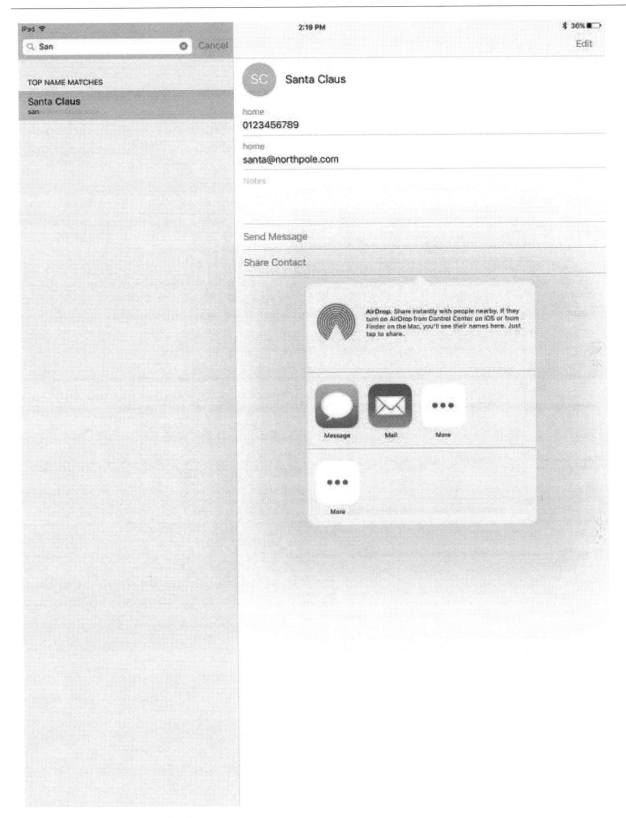

Figure 3: Contact Info Screen

3. Deleting a Contact

You may delete contact information from your phonebook in order to free up space, or for organizational purposes. To delete unwanted contact information:

Warning: There is no way to restore contact information after it has been deleted.

1. Touch the ![icon] icon on the Home screen. The phonebook appears.
2. Touch the name of the contact that you wish to delete. The Contact Info screen appears. Refer to *"Finding a Contact"* on page 33 to learn how to search for a contact.
3. Touch **Edit** at the top of the screen. The Contact Information Editing screen appears.
4. Scroll down, and touch **Delete Contact** at the bottom of the screen, as shown in **Figure 4**. A Confirmation menu appears.
5. Touch **Delete Contact** again. The contact's information is deleted, and no longer appears in your phonebook.

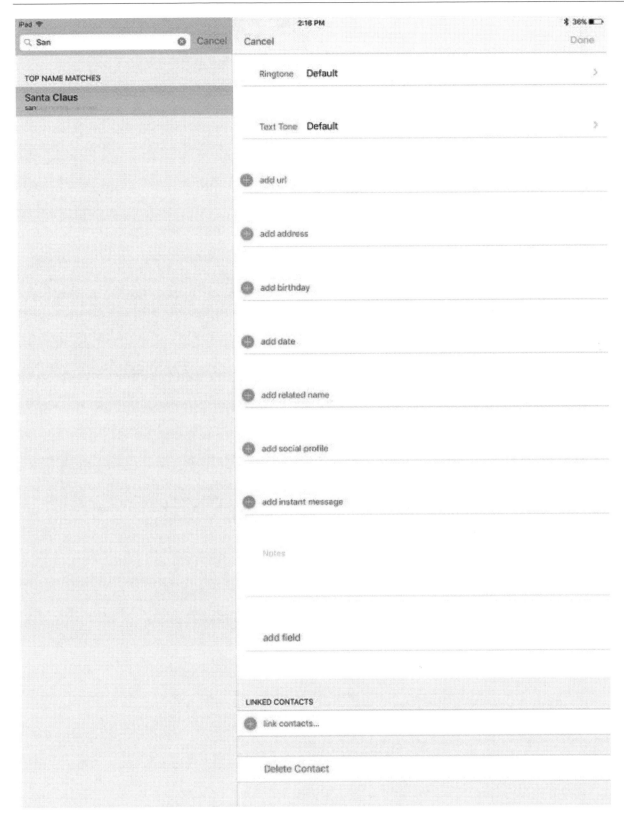

Figure 4: Delete Contact Screen

4. Editing Contact Information

After adding contacts to your phonebook, you may edit them at any time. To edit an existing contact's information:

1. Touch the ![icon] icon on the Home screen. The phonebook appears.

2. Touch a contact's name. The Contact Info screen appears. Refer to *"Finding a Contact"* on page 33 to learn how to search for a contact.

3. Touch **Edit** at the top of the screen. The Contact Editing screen appears.

4. Touch a field to edit the corresponding information. Touch **Done** at the top of the screen when you are finished. The contact's information is updated.

5. Sharing a Contact's Information

To share a contact's information with someone else:

1. Touch the ![icon] icon. The phonebook appears.
2. Touch a contact's name. The Contact Info screen appears. Refer to *"Finding a Contact"* on page 33 to learn how.
3. Touch **Share Contact** at the bottom of the contact's information. The Sharing Options menu appears, as shown in **Figure 5**.
4. Follow the steps in the appropriate section below to email or text the contact's information:

To send the contact's information via email:

1. Touch the ![icon] icon in the Sharing Options menu. The New Email screen appears with the contact's information attached, as shown in **Figure 6**. Choose one of the following options for entering the email address:

- Start typing the name of the contact with whom you wish to share the information. The matching contacts appear. Touch the contact's name. The contact's email address is added.

- Enter the email address from scratch. To use a number, touch the **.?123** button at the bottom left of the screen. When done, touch the **return** button in the lower right-hand corner of the screen. Enter more addresses if needed.

- Touch the ⊕ icon to select contacts from your phonebook, or enter as many email addresses as you wish.

2. Enter an optional subject by touching **Subject**, and touch **CC** to add other addresses to which to send the information.

3. Touch **Send** at the top of the screen. The contact's information is sent to the selected email addresses.

To send a contact's information via multimedia message, touch the icon in the Sharing Options menu. The New Message screen appears with the contact's information attached, as shown in **Figure 7**. Enter the phone number or phone numbers, and touch **Send**. The contact's information is sent. There are three methods for entering the phone number:

- Start typing the name of the contact with whom you wish to share the information. Matching contacts appear. Touch the contact's name. The contact's number is added.

- Type the phone number from scratch. To use numbers, touch the **.?123** button at the bottom of the screen. When done, touch **return** on the right side of the screen.

- Touch the ⊕ icon to select one or more contacts from the phonebook.

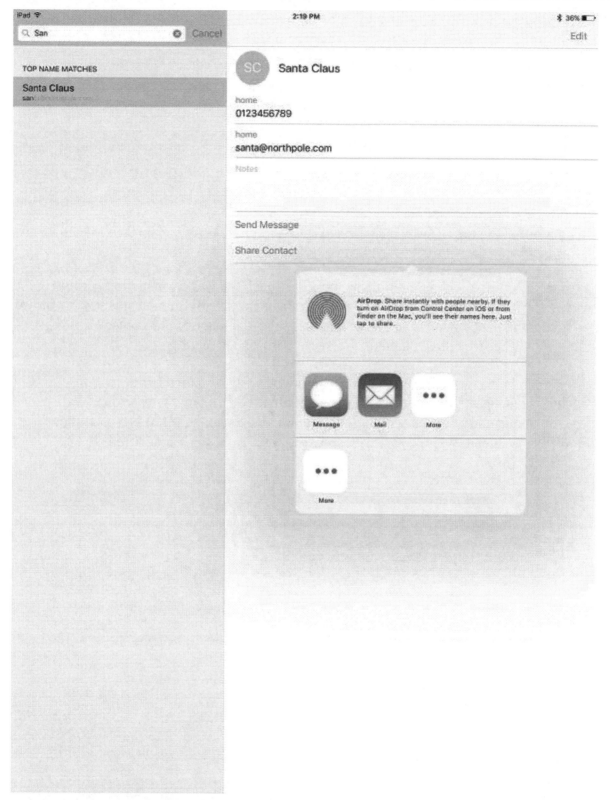

Figure 5: Sharing Options Menu

Figure 6: New Email Screen

Figure 7: New Message Screen

6. Changing the Contact Sort Order

By default, the iPad sorts the contacts in the phonebook by last name. For instance, if the names Jane Doe and John Johnson are in the phonebook, John Johnson would come after Jane Doe because 'J' comes after 'D' in the English alphabet. To change the sort order:

1. Touch the ⚙ icon. The Settings screen appears, as shown in **Figure 8**.
2. Scroll down, and touch **Mail, Contacts, Calendars**. The Mail, Contacts, Calendars screen appears, as shown in **Figure 9**.
3. Scroll down, and touch **Sort Order**. The Sort Order screen appears, as shown in **Figure 10**.
4. Touch **First, Last**. A check mark appears to the right of the option, and the contacts are sorted by first name.
5. Touch **Last, First**. A check mark appears to the right of the option, and the contacts are sorted by last name.

Figure 8: Settings Screen

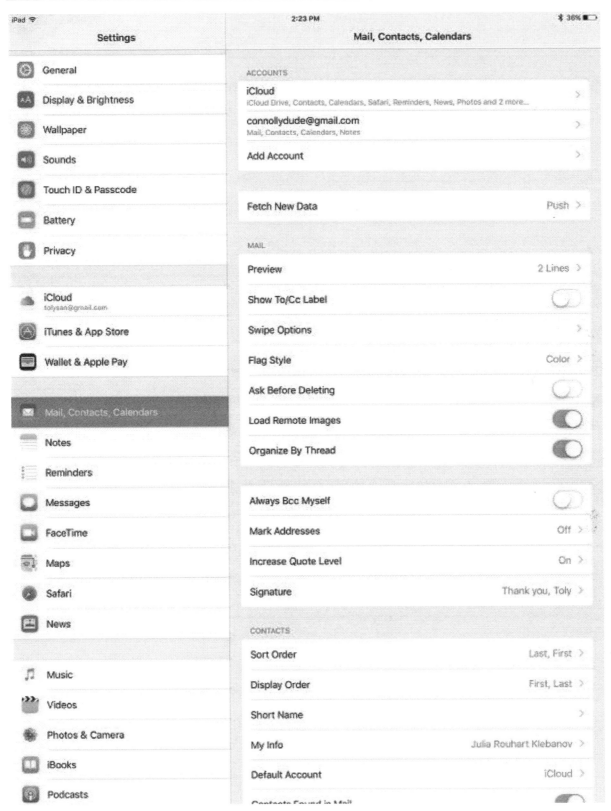

Figure 9: Mail, Contacts, Calendars Screen

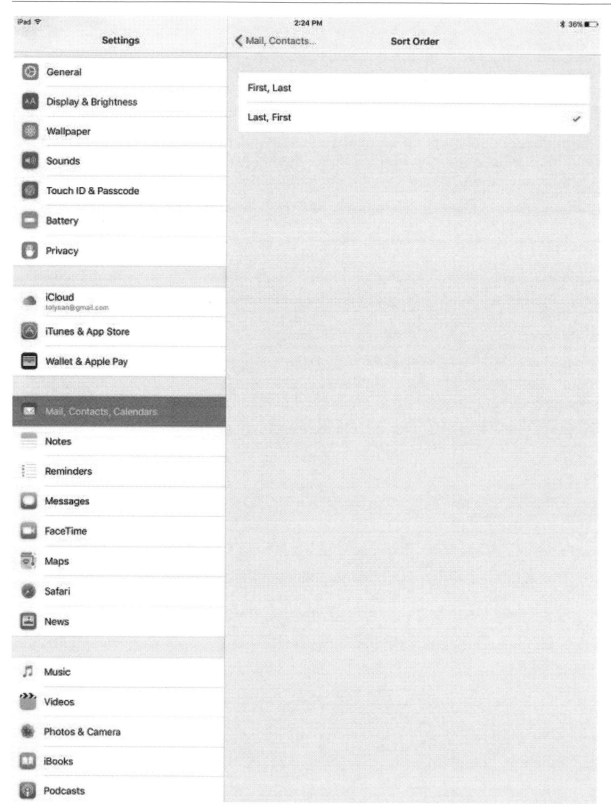

Figure 10: Sort Order Screen

Text Messaging

Table of Contents

1. Turning On and Registering with iMessage

Unlike the iPhone, the iPad does not allow you to send text messages until you turn on iMessage and log in using your Apple ID. To turn on and register with iMessage:

1. Touch the ![icon] icon. The Settings screen appears, as shown in **Figure 1**.
2. Scroll down and touch **Messages**. The Message Settings screen appears, as shown in **Figure 2**.
3. Enter the email address and password associated with your Apple ID, and touch **Sign In**. iMessage is registered, and a list of previously registered email addresses (if any) appears, as shown in **Figure 3**.
4. Touch **Next** at the top of the screen. The iMessage registration is complete. If you want to register additional email addresses, touch **Send & Receive** on the Message Settings screen.

Figure 1: Settings Screen

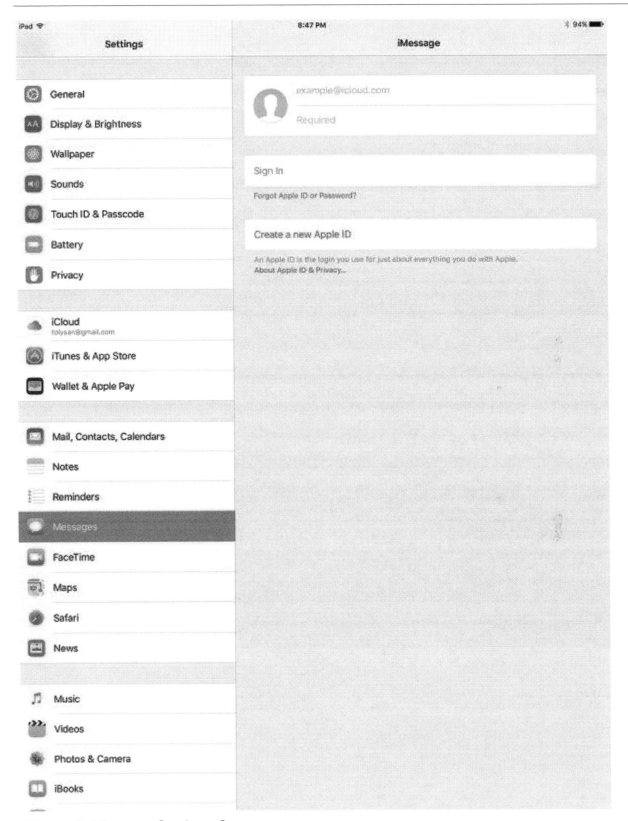

Figure 2: Message Settings Screen

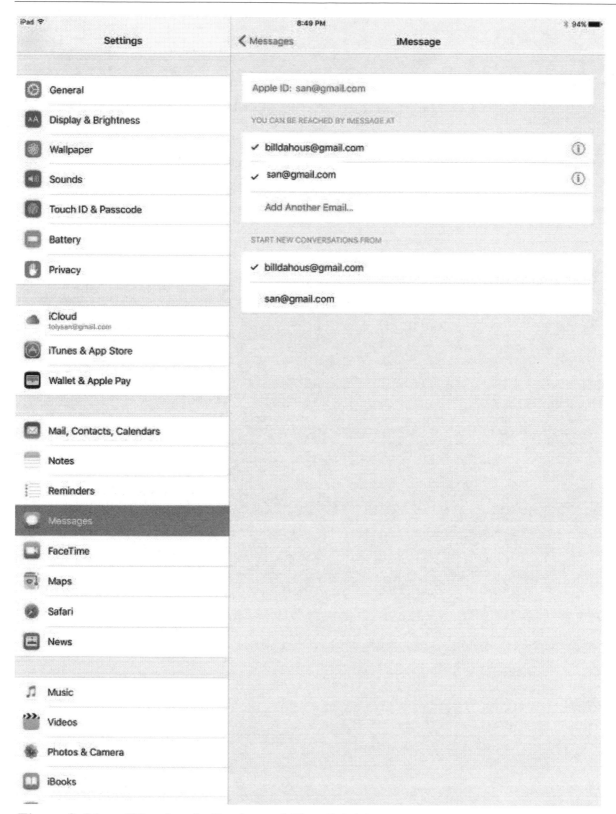

Figure 3: List of Previously Registered Email Addresses

2. Composing a New Text Message

The iPad can send text messages to other iPads, iPhones, and Macs. To compose a new message:

1. Touch the icon on the Home screen. The Messages screen appears, as shown in **Figure 4**.

2. Touch the icon at the top of the screen. The New Message screen appears, as shown in **Figure 5**.

3. Enter the phone number or email address of the recipient. The recipient must be using iMessage to receive your text message. There are three options for entering this information:

   - Start typing the name of the contact. Matching contacts appear as you type. Touch the contact's name. The contact's number is added.

   - Enter the phone number from scratch.

   - Touch the button to select a contact from the Phonebook. Add as many numbers as desired.

4. Touch the text field. The cursor starts flashing at the beginning of the field.

5. Enter your message. If you begin to type a word incorrectly, the iPad may give you a suggestion. To accept the suggestion, touch **Space**. To reject it, touch the key. The iPad also suggests words to complete a sentence based on what you have typed in the past.

6. Touch **Send** when finished. The message is sent. Your message is shown in a blue bubble on the right side of the screen, as shown in **Figure 6**. All text messages are shown in conversation view.

To send a new message to someone you have already texted:

1. Touch the icon on the Home screen. The Messages screen appears.

2. Touch the name or number of the recipient. The Conversation screen appears. If the name is not in the list, try scrolling down by touching the screen and moving your finger up. If you cannot find the name, you may have deleted your conversation with that contact.

3. Touch the text field. The cursor starts flashing, and a keyboard is shown.

4. Enter the message and then touch **Send**. The message is sent. The most recent message is shown in a blue bubble. Touch the screen and move your finger down to scroll through older messages.

Figure 4: Messages Screen

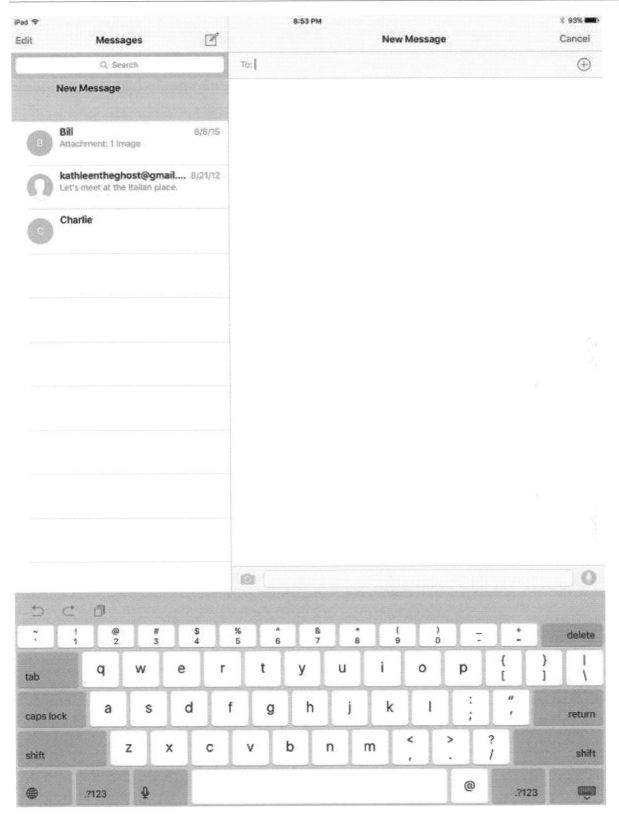

Figure 5: New Message Screen

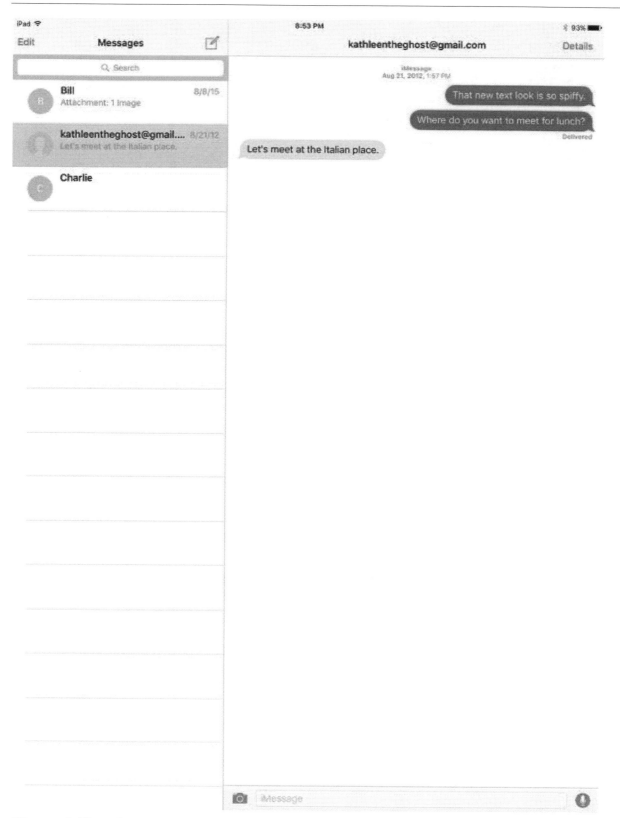

Figure 6: Your Message in a Blue Bubble

3. Copying, Cutting, and Pasting Text

The iPad allows you to copy or cut text from one location and paste it to another. Copying leaves the text in its current location and allows you to paste it elsewhere. Cutting deletes the text from its current location and allows you to paste it elsewhere. To cut, copy, and paste text:

1. Touch and hold text in a text field, or in a conversation. The Select menu appears above the text, as shown in **Figure 7**. Refer to *"Composing a New Text Message"* on page 51 to learn how to compose a text.
2. Touch **Select All**. All of the text is selected. To select a single word, touch **Select**. Blue dots appear around the word or phrase.
3. Touch and hold one of the blue dots and drag it in any direction. The text between the dots is highlighted and a text menu appears, as shown in **Figure 8**.
4. Touch **Cut** or **Copy**. The corresponding action is taken, and the text is ready to be pasted.
5. Touch and hold any empty text field, and then touch **Paste**. The text is inserted.

Note: Refer to "Tips and Tricks" *on page 302 to learn more about editing text.*

Figure 7: Select Menu

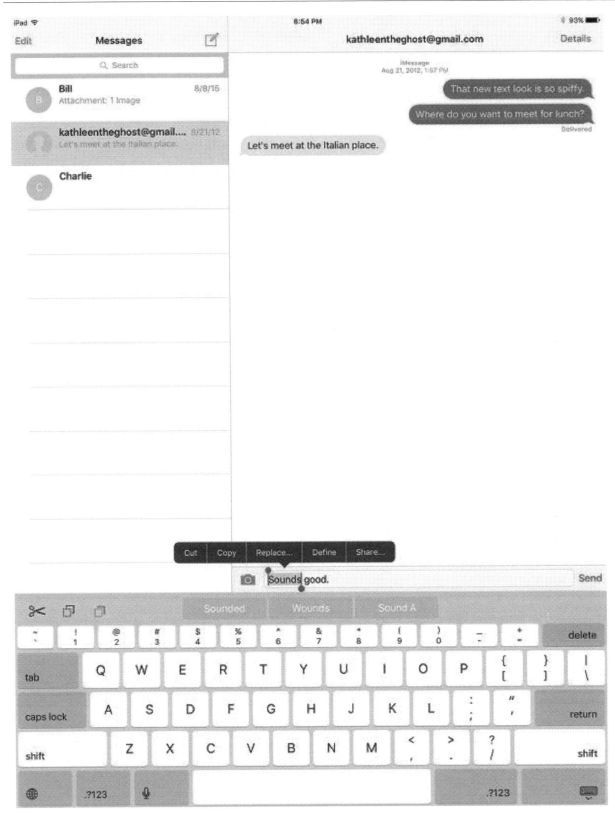

Figure 8: Text Menu

4. Using the Spell Check Feature

The iPad makes suggestions for words that are spelled incorrectly. Touch a suggestion to substitute the word immediately. If auto-correction is enabled, the iPad automatically replaces common typos. Over time, the iPad learns your most commonly typed words, even names and slang. Refer to *"Adjusting Language and Keyboard Settings"* on page 225 to learn more about auto-correction.

5. Receiving a Text Message

The iPad can receive text messages from any other iPad, iPhone (with iMessage enabled), or Mac (with iMessage enabled). When the iPad receives a text it plays a specific sound, which depends on the settings. The New Message notification appears on the Lock screen, as shown in **Figure 9**, on the Home screen, as shown in **Figure 10**, or in the Notification Bar at the top of the screen, as outlined in **Figure 11**. Whether the notification appears in the Notification Bar or on the Home screen depends on your settings. Use the following tips when receiving text messages:

- Slide the icon to the right on the Lock screen to open the text message.

- Slide the Notification Bar down while running an application. The Quick Message Reply window appears, as shown in **Figure 12**. To reply without opening the Messages application, enter a reply and touch **Send**.

- The icon next to the icon on the Home screen indicates that there is one unread message. This number changes depending on the number of unread messages. The number in the red circle does not disappear until the message is read. Touch the icon to view the message.

If the New Message notification appears on the Home screen, or while you are using an application:

- Touch **Reply** to send a quick text back to the contact without opening the Messages application.

- Touch **Close** to reply later.

Note: Refer to "Composing a New Text Message" *on page 51 to learn more about sending text messages. Refer to* "Adjusting Sound Settings" *on page 218 to learn how to change the New Message notification sound.*

Figure 9: New Message Notification on the Lock Screen

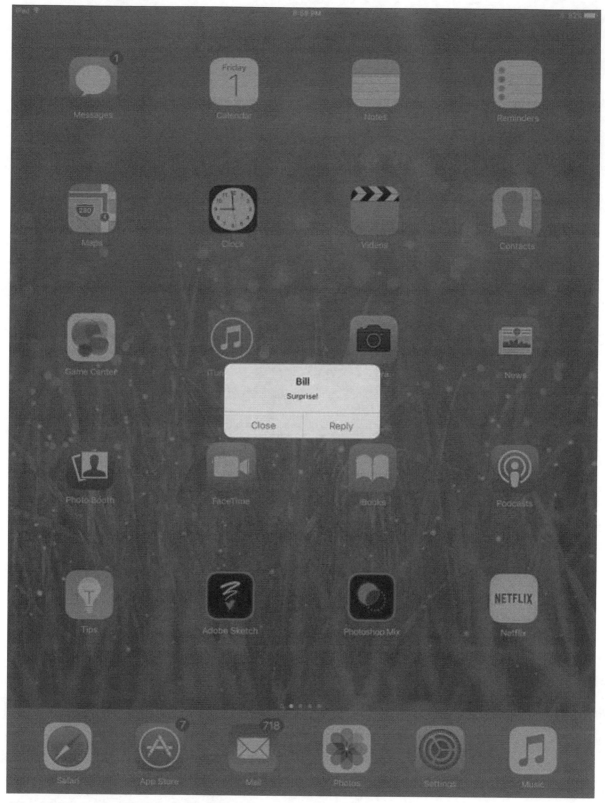

Figure 10: New Message Notification on the Home Screen

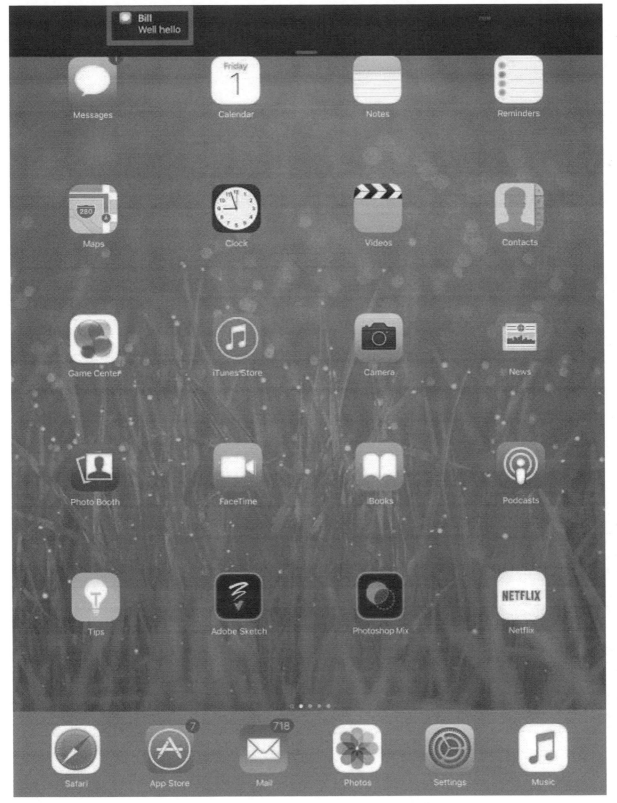

Figure 11: New Message Notification in the Notification Bar

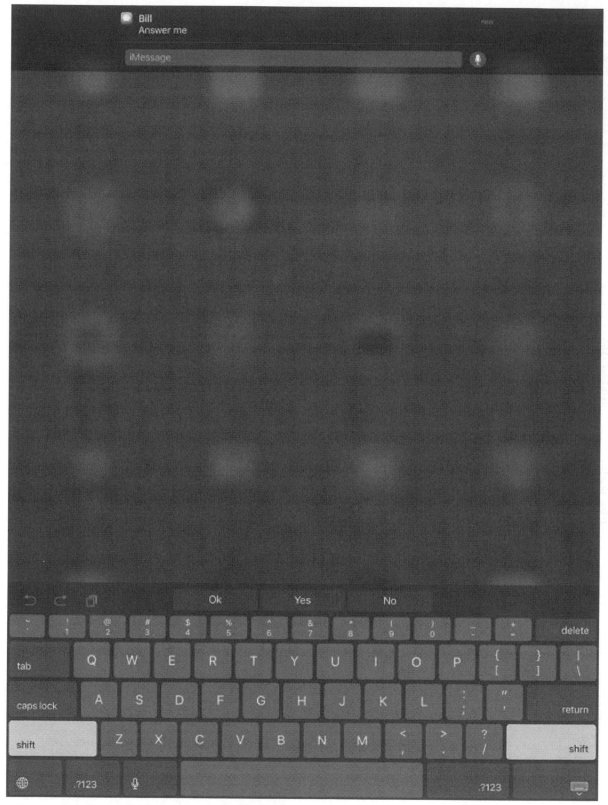

Figure 12: Quick Message Reply Window

6. Reading a Stored Text Message

You may read any text messages that you have received, provided that you have not deleted them. To read stored text messages:

1. Touch the ▢ icon on the Home screen. The Messages screen appears. The iPad organizes conversations based on the date the last message in the conversation was sent or received, with the most recent conversation at the top of the list.
2. Touch the name of a contact to view the conversation. The Conversation screen appears.
3. Touch the screen, and move your finger up or down to scroll through the conversation. The most recent messages appear at the bottom.

7. Forwarding a Text Message

Forwarding a message copies the contents of the original message when you wish to send it to a new recipient. You may wish to forward a text message to save yourself some time entering the same message. To forward a text message:

1. Touch the ▢ icon on the Home screen. The Messages screen appears, displaying each sender's name on the left and the date of the message on the right.
2. Touch the conversation that contains the message(s) that you wish to forward. The Conversation screen appears.
3. Touch and hold a message in the conversation. The Message menu appears above the message.
4. Touch **More**. A blue check mark appears next to the message, as shown in **Figure 13**.
5. Touch the ⤳ button at the bottom of the screen. The New Message screen appears, with the selected message copied into the text field.
6. Start typing the name of a contact or touch the ⊕ icon to select a number from the Phonebook. The contact is added to the Addressee list.
7. Touch **Send**. The message is forwarded to the contacts in the 'To:' field.

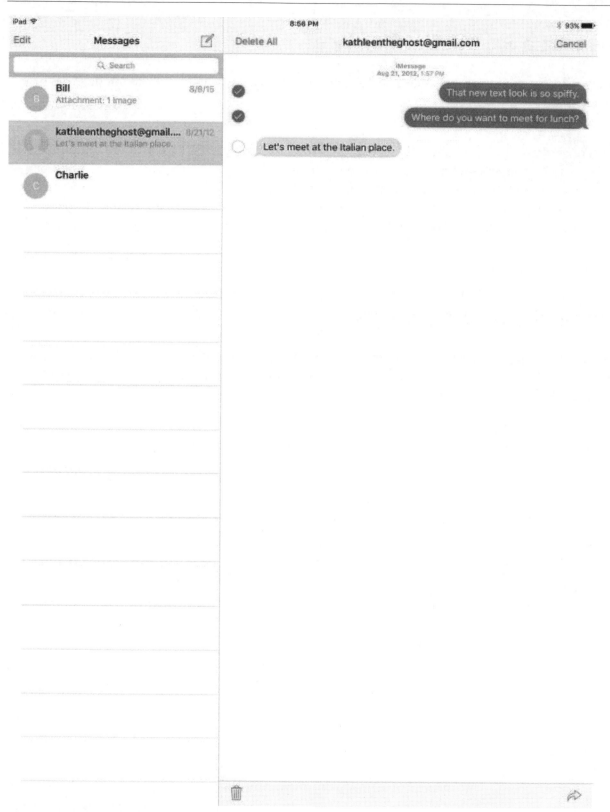

Figure 13: Selected Messages

8. Viewing Sender Information from within a Text

If you have stored a contact's information in the Phonebook, you may view it at any time without leaving a text conversation between the two of you. To view the information of a contact who sent you a message:

1. Touch the [icon] icon on the Home screen. The Messages screen appears.
2. Touch a conversation. The Conversation screen appears.
3. Touch the screen and move your finger down until the top of the conversation appears.
4. Touch **Details** at the top of the screen. The Conversation Details screen appears.
5. Touch the (i) icon. The Contact Information screen appears.

9. Deleting a Text Message

The iPad can delete separate text messages or an entire conversation, which is a series of text messages between you and a contact.

Warning: Once deleted, text messages cannot be restored.

To delete an entire conversation:

1. Touch the [icon] icon on the Home screen. The Messages screen appears.
2. Touch and hold a message in a conversation. The Message menu appears.
3. Touch **More**. A [check mark] mark appears next to the selected message.
4. Touch **Delete All** at the top of the screen. A confirmation dialog appears.
5. Touch **Delete Conversation**. The entire conversation is deleted.

To delete a separate text message:

1. Touch the [icon] icon on the Home screen. The Messages screen appears.
2. Touch and hold a message in a conversation. The message menu appears.
3. Touch **More**. Touch any other messages that you wish to delete. A [check mark] mark appears next to each selected message.
4. Touch the [trash] icon at the bottom of the screen. A confirmation dialog appears.

5. Touch **Delete Message**. The selected messages are deleted.

10. Adding Texted Phone Numbers to the Phonebook

A phone number sent via text message can be added to your Phonebook immediately. To add a texted phone number to your Phonebook:

1. Touch the ⬜ icon on the Home screen. The Messages screen appears.
2. Touch a conversation. The Conversation screen appears.
3. Touch and hold the phone number in the conversation for two seconds. The Phone Number menu appears, as shown in **Figure 14**. On an iPad, the Phone Number menu appears above the phone number.
4. Touch **Add to Contacts**. The Info screen appears.
5. Touch **Create New Contact** or **Add to Existing Contact**. If you touched 'Create New Contact', the New Contact screen appears, with the phone number field filled in, as shown in **Figure 15**. If you touched 'Add to Existing Contact', the phonebook appears. Select a contact's name, to which you wish to assign the new number.
6. Touch **First** and enter a first name. Touch **Last** and enter a last name.
7. Touch **Done**. The contact is added to your Phonebook.

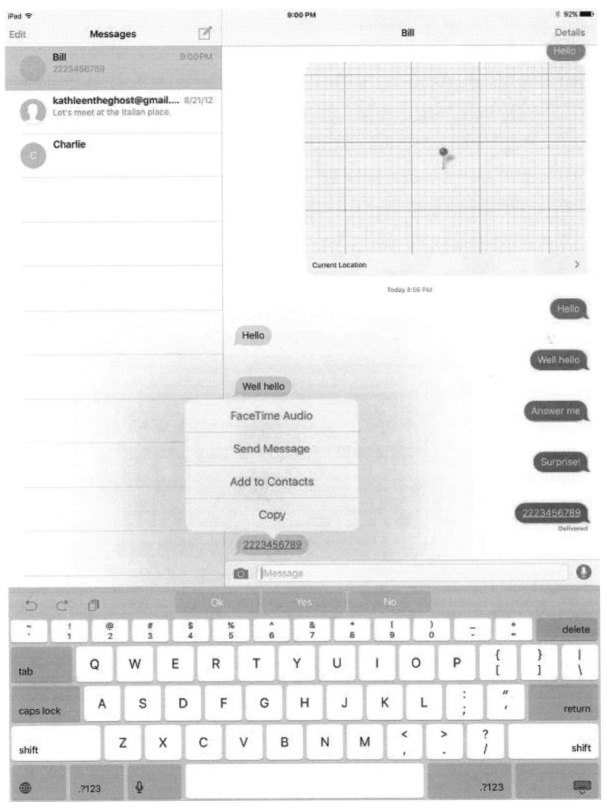

Figure 14: Phone Number Menu

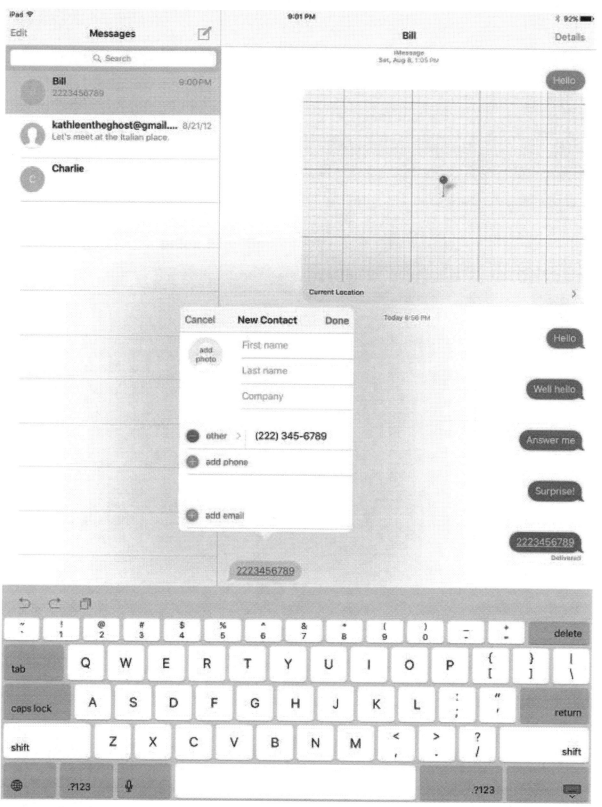

Figure 15: New Contact Screen

11. Sending a Picture Message

You may attach a picture to any text message that you send.
To send a picture message:

1. Touch the ⬜ icon on the Home screen. The Messages screen appears.

2. Touch the ⬜ icon. The New Message screen appears.

3. Touch the 📷 button to the left of the text field. The Photo Attachment menu appears, as shown in **Figure 16**.

4. Follow the steps in one of the sections below to either attach an existing picture or take a picture to send:

To attach an existing picture to the text message:

1. Touch **Photo Library**. A list of Photo Albums appears, as shown in **Figure 17**.
2. Touch a photo album. The photo album opens.
3. Touch a photo. The preview of the photo appears.
4. Touch **Choose**. The photo is attached to the text message. Alternatively, touch **Cancel** to select a different photo.

To take a picture and attach it to the text message:

1. Touch **Take Photo or Video**. The camera turns on, as shown in **Figure 18**.

2. Touch the ⬜ button on the right side of the screen. The photo is captured and a preview of the photo appears.

3. Touch **Use Photo** to use the photo in the message, or touch **Retake** to discard the picture and take another one. The photo is attached. Alternatively, touch **Cancel** while the camera is turned on to return to the conversation without taking a picture.

4. Touch **Send**. The picture message is sent.

Note: Up to nine photos may be sent in a picture message.

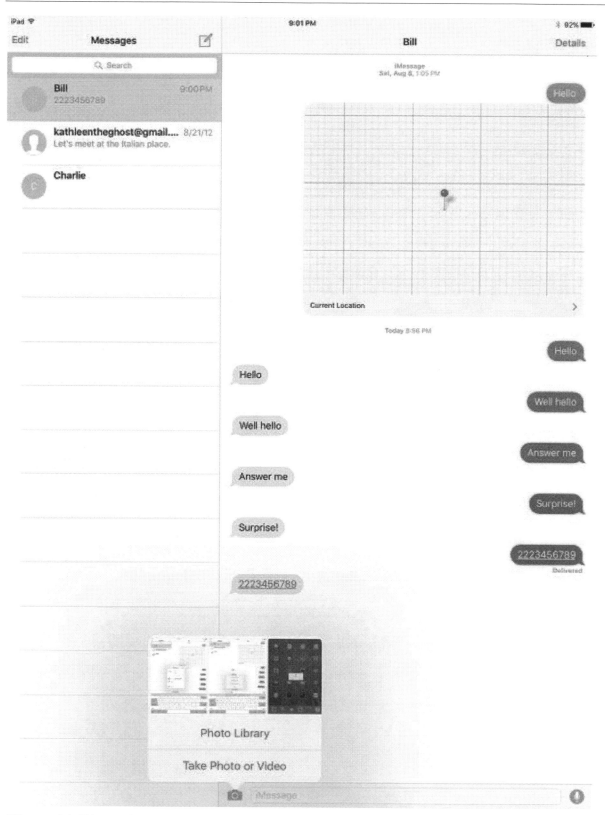

Figure 16: Photo Attachment Menu

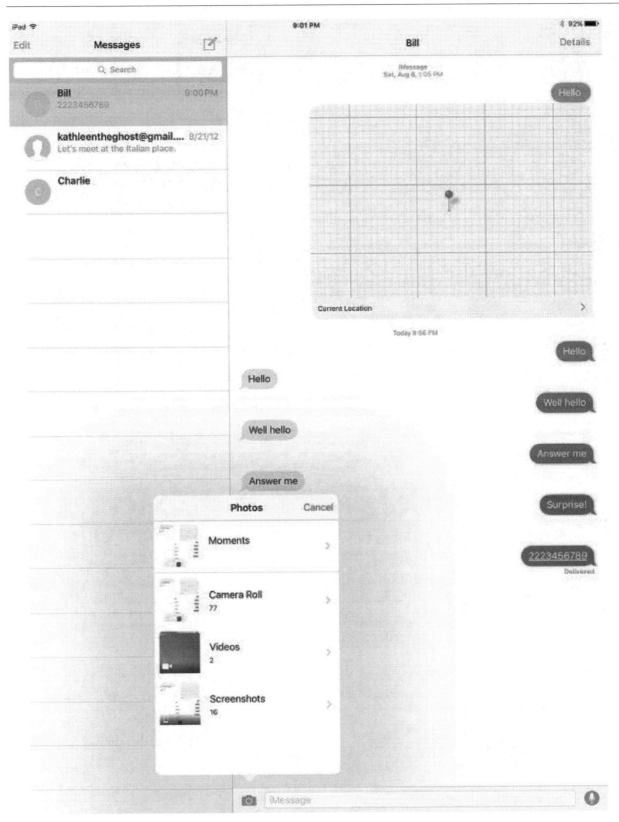

Figure 17: List of Photo Albums

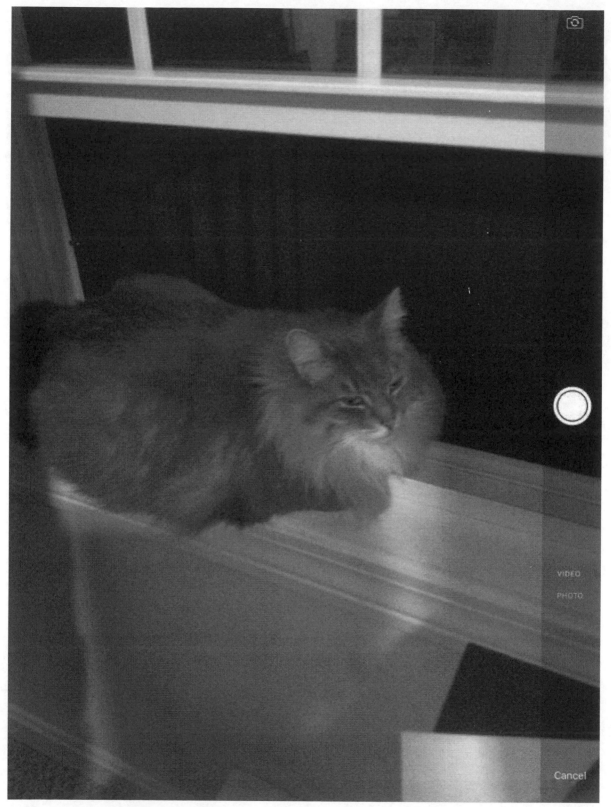

Figure 18: Camera Turned On

12. Leaving a Group Conversation

You may remove yourself from a group conversation if you no longer wish to participate. Once removed, you do not receive any further messages in that conversation. To leave a group conversation:

1. Touch **Details** at the top of the conversation. The Conversation details appear.
2. Touch **Leave this Conversation**. A confirmation dialog appears.
3. Touch **Leave this Conversation** again. You are removed from the conversation.

13. Adding a Voice Message to a Conversation

You may add a short voice message to a text message or conversation. This feature only works when using iMessage. If you send a text message to someone who does not use an Apple device, or has not registered for iMessage, this feature does not work. To add a voice message to an iMessage:

1. Touch and hold the icon to the right of the text field. The microphone turns on.
2. Speak the voice message that you would like to attach. When you are finished, release the icon. The voice message is recorded, as shown in **Figure 19**.
3. Touch the icon. The voice message is sent. Alternatively, touch the icon to preview the voice message, or touch the icon if you would like to discard the voice message.

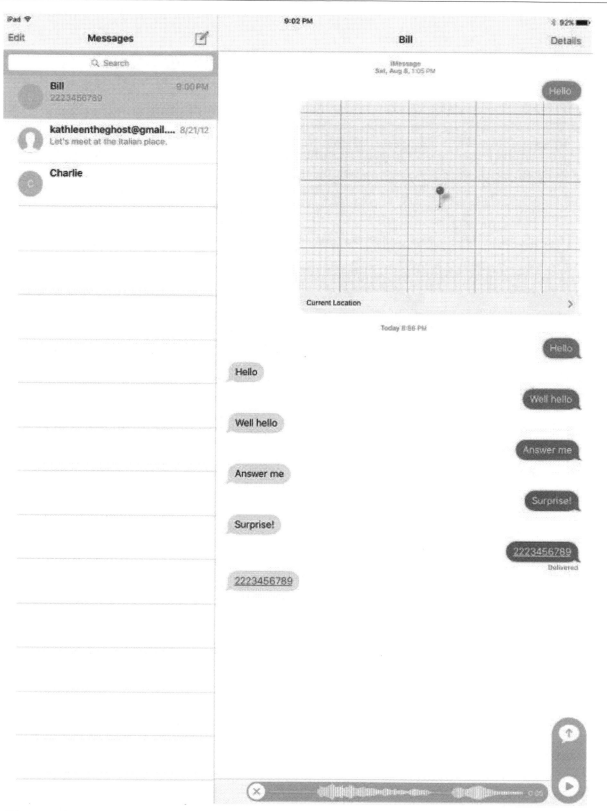

Figure 19: Recorded Voice Message

14. Quickly Adding a Video or Photo to a Conversation

You may quickly add a video to a conversation if you are on the go. To add a video to a conversation:

1. Touch and hold the icon, and drag your finger up. The camera turns on.
2. Drag your finger over **Photo**, and release the screen. The camera captures a picture, and immediately sends it to the recipient.
3. You may also drag your finger over, and hold the icon to record a quick video. Release the icon when you have finished recording. Touch **Send** to send the video.

   Alternatively, touch the icon to preview the video, or touch **Delete** if you would like to discard the video.

15. Sharing Your Location in a Conversation

You may choose to share your location with a contact or a number of participants in a conversation. To share your location for a specified amount of time:

1. Touch **Details** in the upper right-hand corner of the conversation. The Conversation details appear.
2. Touch **Share My Location**. The Location Sharing menu appears, as shown in **Figure 20**.
3. Touch one of the following options to share your location for the corresponding amount of time: **Share for One Hour**, **Share Until End of Day**, or **Share Indefinitely**. Your location is shared. The last option allows you to share your location until you touch **Stop Sharing My Location** on the Conversation Details screen.

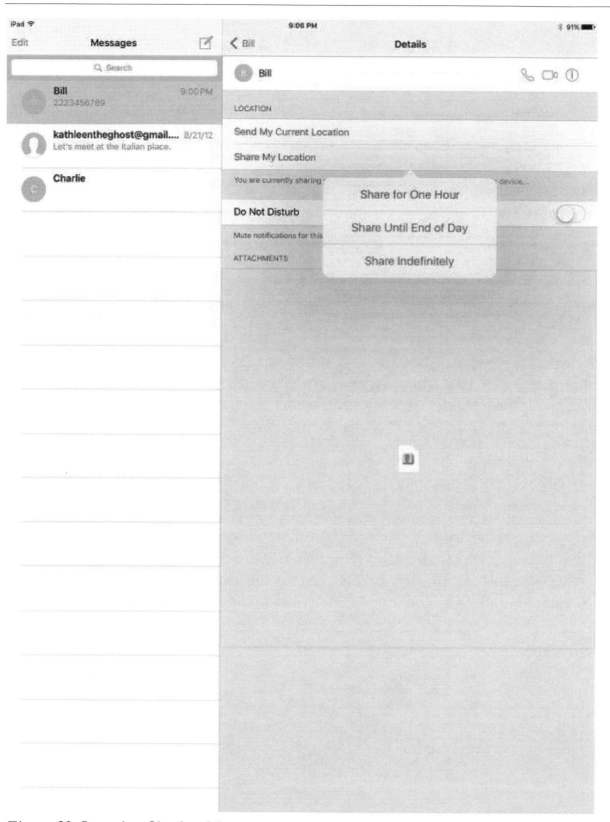

Figure 20: Location Sharing Menu

16. Viewing All Attachments in a Conversation

The Messaging application provides a convenient way to view all of the pictures, videos, and voice messages attached to a conversation in one neat list. To view all attachments in a conversation, touch **Details** at the top of a conversation. The Conversation details appear, and the list of attachments is shown at the bottom of the screen. To save one of the attachments in the list to a photo album:

1. Touch the attachment that you want to save. The attachment appears in full screen.
2. Touch the center of the screen. The Attachment menu appears at the top of the screen, as shown in **Figure 21**.

3. Touch the icon at the top of the screen, if it is a photo, or at the bottom of the screen, if it is a video. The Save Photo menu appears, as shown in **Figure 22**, or the Save Video menu appears, as shown in **Figure 23**.

4. Touch the icon. The attachment is saved to the Recently Added album on your iPad.

Figure 21: Attachment Menu

Figure 22: Save Photo Menu

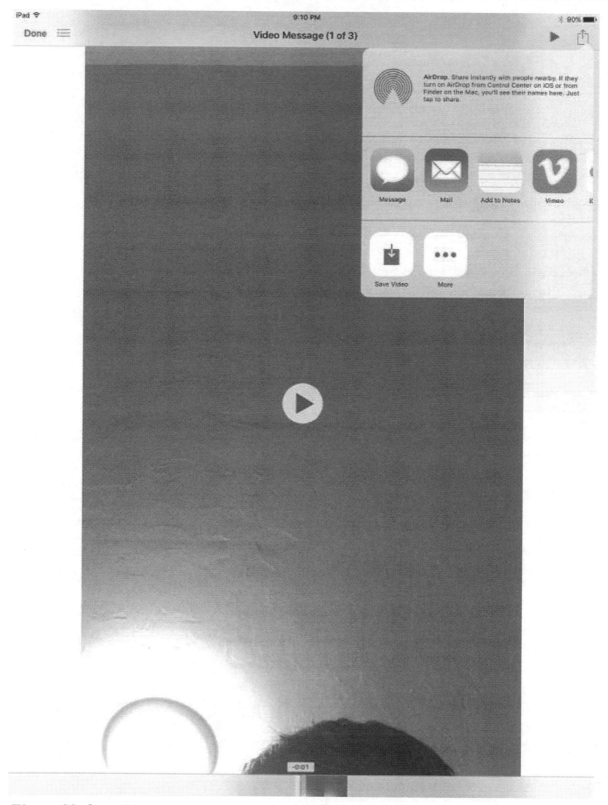

Figure 23: Save Video Menu

Using the Safari Web Browser

Table of Contents

1. Navigating to a Website

You can surf the web using your iPad. To navigate to a website using the web address:

1. Touch the ![icon] icon on the Home screen. The Safari Web browser opens.
2. Touch the Address bar at the top of the screen, as outlined in **Figure 1**. The keyboard appears. If you do not see the Address bar, touch the screen and move your finger down to scroll up.
3. Touch the web address at the top of the screen. button. The address field is erased.
4. Enter a web address and touch **Go**. Safari navigates to the website.
5. Touch the ![<] button. Safari navigates to the previous web page.
6. Touch the ![>] button. Safari navigates to the next web page.

Figure 1: Address Bar in Safari

2. Adding and Viewing Bookmarks

The iPad can store favorite websites as bookmarks to allow you to access them faster in the future. To add a Bookmark in Safari:

1. Touch the [icon] icon on the Home screen. The Safari browser opens.
2. Navigate to a website. Refer to *"Navigating to a Website"* on page 81 to learn how.
3. Touch the [icon] button at the top of the screen. The Bookmark menu appears, as shown in **Figure 2**.
4. Touch the [icon] icon. The Add Bookmark window appears, as shown in **Figure 3**.
5. Enter a name for the bookmark and touch **Save** in the top right-hand corner of the screen. The website is added to the list of bookmarks.
6. To view saved Bookmarks, touch the [icon] icon at the top of the screen. The Bookmarks screen appears, as shown in **Figure 4**. Touch a bookmark. Safari navigates to the indicated website.

Figure 2: Bookmark Menu

Figure 3: Add Bookmark Window

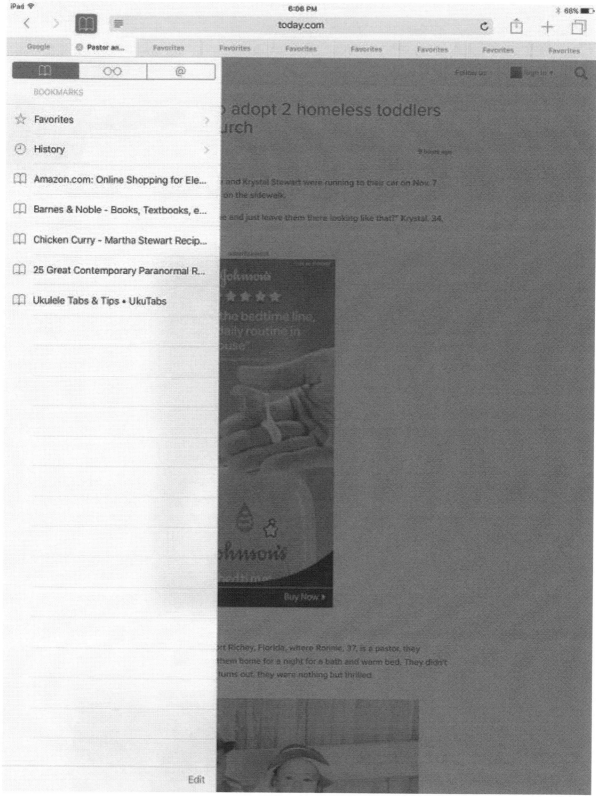

Figure 4: Bookmarks Screen

3. Adding a Bookmark to the Home Screen

On the iPad, bookmarks can be added to the Home screen, which appear like application icons. To add a bookmark to the Home screen as an icon:

1. Touch the ![icon] icon on the Home screen. The Safari browser opens.
2. Navigate to a website. Refer to *"Navigating to a Website"* on page 81 to learn how.
3. Touch the ![icon] button at the top of the screen. The Bookmark menu appears.
4. Touch the ![icon] icon. The Add to Home window appears, as shown in **Figure 5**.
5. Enter a name for the bookmark and touch **Add**. The bookmark is added to the Home screen.

Figure 5: Add to Home Window

4. Managing Open Browser Tabs

The Safari Web browser supports up to 36 open browser tabs. This feature is analogous to tabbed browsing in a browser like Mozilla Firefox or Google Chrome. Use the following tips when working with browser tabs:

To view the open Safari tabs, touch the ⬜ button. The open Safari tabs appear, as shown in **Figure 6**. Touch the screen and flick your finger up or down to view other open tabs. While viewing the open Safari tabs:

- To open a new browser tabs, touch the ➕ button.
- To close a tab, touch the tab and move it to the left. You can also touch **Done** to return to the tab that you were just viewing.
- To reorder the tabs, touch and hold a tab, and move it up or down.

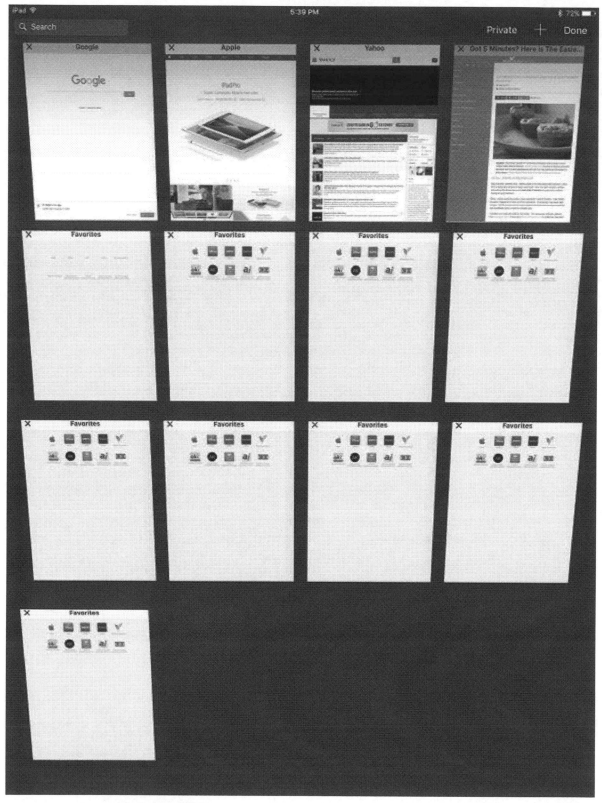

Figure 6: Open Safari Tabs

5. Blocking Pop-Up Windows

Some websites may have pop-up windows that interfere with browsing the internet. By default, pop-ups are already blocked. To block pop-ups:

1. Touch the ⚙ icon on the Home screen. The Settings screen appears, as shown in **Figure 7**.
2. Scroll down and touch **Safari**. The Safari Settings screen appears, as shown in **Figure 8**.
3. Touch the ⬜ switch next to 'Block Pop-Ups'. Pop-ups are blocked.
4. Touch the ⬛ switch next to 'Block Pop-Ups'. Pop-ups are allowed.

Figure 7: Settings Screen

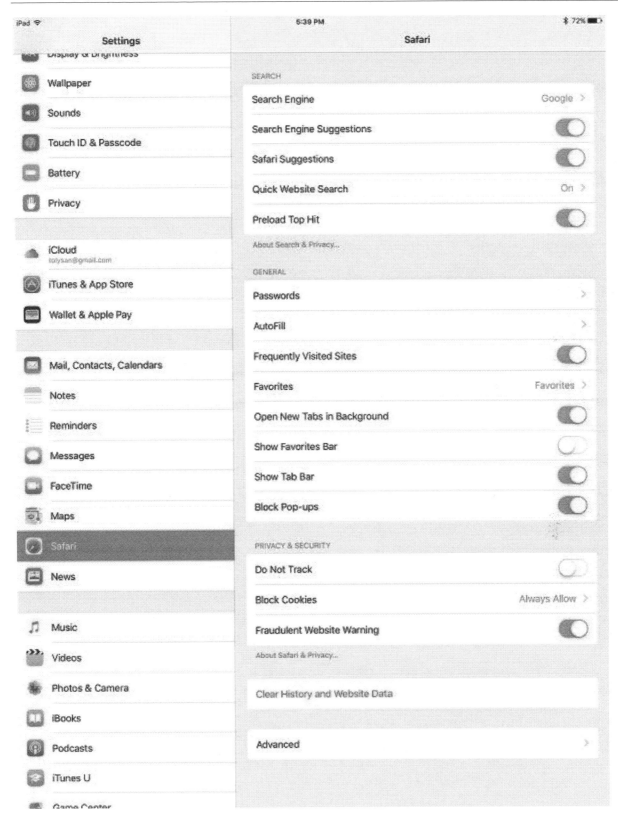

Figure 8: Safari Settings Screen

6. Changing the Search Engine

Google, Yahoo, Bing, Yandex, or DuckDuckGo can be set as the default search engine in Safari. When you get your new iPad, the default search engine is set to Google. The Address bar at the top of the screen also acts as a search field in Safari. To change the default search engine:

1. Touch the ⬤ icon on the Home screen. The Settings screen appears.
2. Touch **Safari**. The Safari Settings screen appears.
3. Touch **Search Engine**. A list of search engines appears.
4. Touch the preferred search engine. The default search engine is set, and its name appears in the empty search field.

7. Clearing the History and Browsing Data

The iPad can clear the list of recently visited websites, known as the History, as well as other data, such as saved passwords, known as Cookies. The iPad can also delete data from previously visited websites, known as the Cache. To delete all of these items:

1. Touch the ⬤ icon on the Home screen. The Settings screen appears.
2. Touch **Safari**. The Safari Settings screen appears.
3. Touch **Clear History and Website Data**. A confirmation dialog appears.
4. Touch **Clear**. The selected data is deleted and the option is grayed out on the Safari Settings screen.

8. Viewing an Article in Reader Mode

The Safari browser can display certain news articles in Reader Mode, which allows you to read them like a book with no images or links. To view an article in Reader Mode, touch the ≡ button in the address bar (when available), as outlined in **Figure 9**. Reader Mode turns on, as shown in **Figure 10**. When Reader Mode is available, "Reader Mode Available" briefly appears in the address bar when the page has finished loading.

Pastor and wife plan to adopt 2 homeless toddlers found outside their church

Alexandra Zaslow
TODAY

9 hours ago

In an effort to beat an incoming storm, Ronnie and Krystal Stewart were running to their car on Nov. 7 when they noticed two young homeless boys on the sidewalk.

"As parents of three kids, how do you go home and just leave them there looking like that?" Krystal, 34, told TODAY.com.

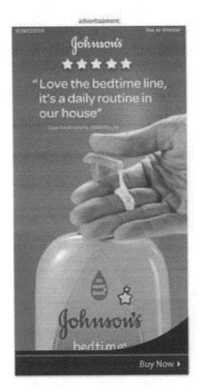

So they didn't.

In the parking lot of Refuge Church in New Port Richey, Florida, where Ronnie, 37, is a pastor, they approached the boys' parents asking to take them home for a night for a bath and warm bed. They didn't know what their response would be, but as it turns out, they were nothing but thrilled.

Figure 9: Reader Button in the Address Bar

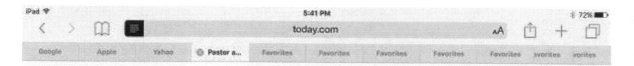

Pastor and wife plan to adopt 2 homeless toddlers found outside their church

In an effort to beat an incoming storm, Ronnie and Krystal Stewart were running to their car on Nov. 7 when they noticed two young homeless boys on the sidewalk.

"As parents of three kids, how do you go home and just leave them there looking like that?" Krystal, 34, told TODAY.com.

So they didn't.

In the parking lot of Refuge Church in New Port Richey, Florida, where Ronnie, 37, is a pastor, they approached the boys' parents asking to take them home for a night for a bath and warm bed. They didn't know what their response would be, but as it turns out, they were nothing but thrilled.

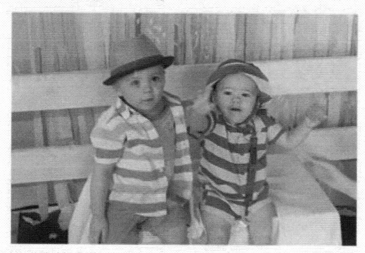

Courtesy of Krystal Stewart

The two boys who will soon legally become part of the Stewart family.

RELATED: Mother reunites with daughter who was placed for adoption 82 years ago

The Stewarts grabbed a playpen and twin mattress from the church and took them home, where they slept for over a straight 10 hours.

"I don't think they've ever slept in a bed before," Krystal said.

Figure 10: Article in Reader Mode

9. Turning Private Browsing On or Off

In order to preserve privacy, the Safari Web browser allows you to surf the internet without saving the History or any other data showing that you have visited a particular website. To open a private tab:

1. Touch the ⬜ button. The open browser tabs appear.
2. Touch **Private**. Private Mode is turned on.
3. Touch the ➕ icon to open a new private tab.
4. When you are ready to exit private mode, touch the ⬜ button, and then touch **Private** again. Safari returns to regular browsing.

10. Setting Up the AutoFill Feature

Safari can automatically fill in personal information, such as passwords and credit card information, to save you time when filling forms or shopping online. To set up the AutoFill feature:

1. Touch the ⚙ icon on the Home screen. The Settings screen appears.
2. Touch **Safari**. The Safari Settings screen appears.
3. Touch **AutoFill**. The Autofill screen appears, as shown in **Figure 11**.
4. Touch one of the following ⬭ switches turn on the corresponding AutoFill:
   - **Use Contact Info** - Enables the use of contact information when filling in forms. The Phonebook appears. Touch the name of a contact to use the contact information to fill in forms. It is recommended that you create a contact entry for yourself and use it for this feature.
   - **Names and Passwords** - Enables the use of saved names and passwords. You have the option to set up a security lock in order to keep your private information safe. Websites give you the option to save your username and password. You can also touch the ⬭ switch next to 'Always Allow' to save passwords even for websites that never save your password.
   - **Credit Cards** - Enables the use of saved credit card information. You have the option to set up a security lock in order to keep your private information safe. Touch **Saved Credit Cards**, and then touch **Add Credit Card** to add a new credit card.

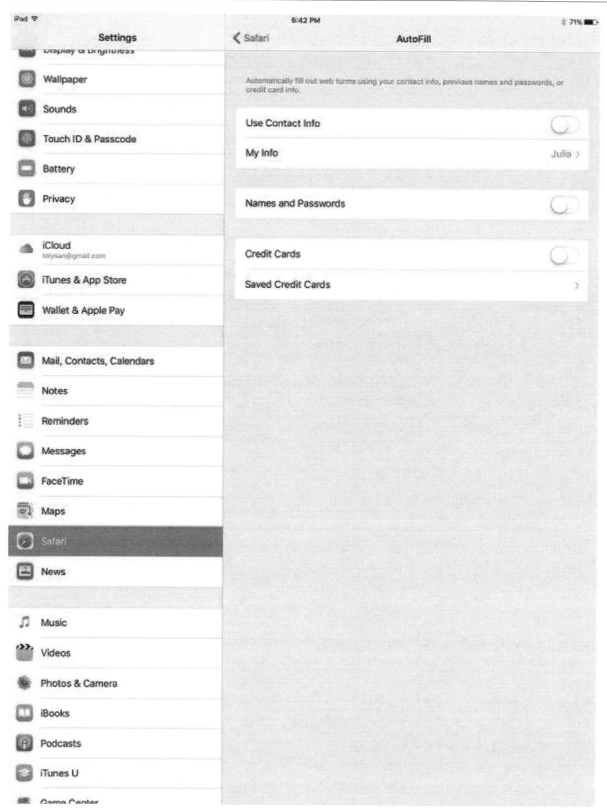

Figure 11: Autofill Screen

11. Customizing the Smart Search Field

The address bar in the Safari browser can act as a search field that assists you by matching your search terms while you type. To customize the smart search field:

1. Touch the ⊚ icon on the Home screen. The Settings screen appears.
2. Touch **Safari**. The Safari Settings screen appears.
3. Touch one of the following ⬭ switches to turn on the corresponding smart search feature:
   - **Search Engine Suggestions** - Enables search term matching to assist you when performing a search.
   - **Preload Top Hit** - Automatically loads the most popular search result when you perform a search. The web page is loaded in the background before you even touch the link.

Note: Refer to "Changing the Search Engine" *on page 94 to learn how to customize the search engine in Safari.*

12. Viewing Recently Closed Tabs

The Safari browser saves a history of all browser tabs that were recently closed. To view all recently closed browser tabs:

1. Touch the ◉ icon on the Home screen. The Safari Web browser opens.
2. Touch and hold the ➕ icon. A list of recently closed browser tabs appears, as shown in **Figure 12**.
3. Touch one of the websites in the list. The selected website opens in a new tab.

Figure 12: List of Recently Closed Tabs

13. Scanning a Credit Card Using the iPad's Camera

When you wish to use a credit card to purchase a product online, you have the option to use your iPad's camera to scan the card. To scan a credit card using the camera:

1. Navigate to the website where you wish to enter the credit card number. Refer to *"Navigating to a Website"* on page 81 to learn how.
2. Touch the credit card field on the page. The virtual keyboard appears.
3. Touch **Scan Credit Card** above the keyboard. The camera turns on. If the Camera Access dialog appears, touch **OK** to allows Safari to use the camera.
4. Align the credit card with the white frame on the screen. The camera reads the credit card number, and enters it in the field.

Note: Use the keyboard to enter the expiration date and security code (on the back of your card).

Managing Photos and Videos

Table of Contents

1. Taking a Picture

The iPad has built-in rear-facing and front-facing cameras. To take a picture, touch the ![icon] icon on the Home screen. The camera turns on, as shown in **Figure 1**. Use the following tips when taking a picture:

- Touch **Square** to take a square picture. Touch **Photo** to activate the default camera.

- Touch the ![button] button in the upper right-hand corner of the screen at any time to switch between the cameras.

- Touch the ![button] button to take a picture. The picture is captured, and is automatically stored in the 'All Photos' album.

Note: Refer to "Tips and Tricks" *on page 301 to learn how to take a picture directly from the Lock screen.*

Figure 1: Camera Turned On

2. Capturing a Video

The iPad has a built-in camcorder that can capture HD video. To capture a video:

1. Touch the icon. The camera turns on.
2. Touch **Video** on the right-hand side of the screen. The camcorder turns on.
3. Touch the button. The camera begins to record.
4. Touch the button. The camera stops recording and the video is automatically saved to the 'All Photos' albums.

Note: Touch the thumbnail in the bottom right-hand corner of the screen to preview the video.

3. Using the Digital Zoom

While taking pictures or capturing video, use the camera's built-in Digital Zoom feature if the subject of the photo is far away. The Digital Zoom will not work when recording videos. To zoom in before taking a photo, touch the screen with two fingers and move them apart. The appears at the bottom of the screen, and the camera zooms in. To zoom out before taking a photo, touch the screen with two fingers apart and bring them together. The appears at the bottom of the screen, and the camera zooms out.

Note: Because of its digital nature, the zoom function will not provide the best resolution, and the image may look fuzzy. Try to be as close as possible to the subject of the photo or video.

4. Focusing on a Part of the Screen

While taking pictures, the camera can focus on a particular object or area on the screen. This will adjust the lighting and other elements to make the object or area stand out in the picture. To focus on a specific part of the screen, just touch that area. An orange box appears and the camera focuses.

5. Browsing Photos

After taking photos on your iPad, or transferring them from your computer, you may view them at any time. To view saved photos:

1. Touch the icon on the Home screen. The Photos application opens.
2. Touch **Albums** at the bottom of the screen. A list of photo albums appears, as shown in **Figure 2** . The photos that you have taken using the iPad are in an album called 'Recently Added'.
3. Touch an album. The photos in the album appear.
4. Touch a photo. The photo appears in full screen.
5. Use the following tips when viewing photos:
   - Touch a photo with your thumb and forefinger and move the two fingers apart to zoom in on it. The zoom will center where your fingers were joined.
   - Touch the screen twice quickly to zoom out completely. Touch the photo with your thumb and forefinger spread apart and move the fingers together while touching the photo to zoom out gradually. Move your fingers apart to zoom in.
   - Touch the button at the top of the screen while viewing a photo to return to album view. If the button is not shown, touch the photo once to make the photo menus appear at the top and bottom of the screen.

Figure 2: List of Photo Albums

6. Editing a Photo

The iPad provides advanced photo-editing tools. To edit a photo:

1. Touch the ![icon] icon at the Home screen. The Photos application opens.
2. Touch **Albums** at the bottom of the screen. A list of photo albums appears.
3. Touch an album. The photos in the album appear.
4. Touch a photo. The photo appears in full screen.
5. Touch **Edit** at the top of the screen. The Photo Editing menu appears, as shown in **Figure 3**.
6. Touch one of the following icons to edit the photo:

![icon] - Enhances the quality of the photo. Touch **Done** to save the changes.

![icon] - Allows you to crop or rotate the photo. Touch the corners of the photo and drag the selected portion, as shown in **Figure 4**. Touch **Done** at the bottom of the screen to save the crop. Repeat steps 1-6 above, and touch **Revert** to return the photo to its original appearance. You may also touch the ![icon] icon to rotate the photo.

![icon] - Allows you to add a color effect, such as Mono (grayscale) or Instant (Polaroid) to the photo.

![icon] - Allows you to customize the appearance of the photo by adjusting the amount of light, color, and tone in the photo. These settings are for advanced users only.

![icon] - Removes red-eye from the photo. Touch each red eye in the photo and then touch **Done** to save the changes.

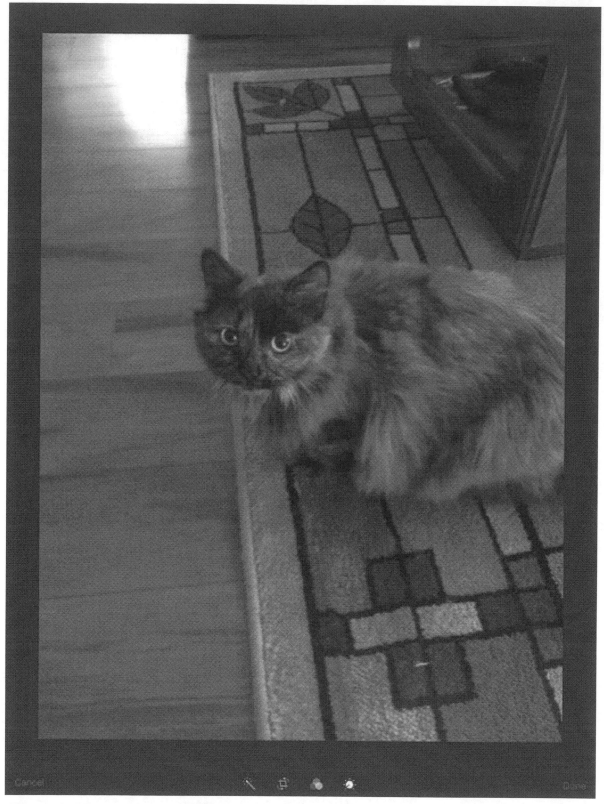

Figure 3: Photo Editing Menu

Figure 4: Cropping a Photo

7. Deleting a Photo

You may delete unwanted pictures from your iPad to free up memory. To delete a photo:

Warning: Once a picture is deleted, there is no way to restore it. Deleting a picture removes it from all albums.

1. Touch the ![icon] icon. The Photos application opens.
2. Touch **Albums** at the bottom of the screen. A list of photo albums appears.
3. Touch an album. The photos contained in the album appear.
4. Touch a photo. The photo appears in full screen view.
5. Touch the ![trash] button at the bottom of the screen. A confirmation dialog appears.
6. Touch **Delete Photo**. The photo is deleted from all albums on the iPad. You may also delete several pictures at a time, by touching **Select** at the top of an album, and then selecting each photo that you wish to delete. Follow steps 5-6 to delete the selected photos.

Note: Refer to "Recovering Deleted Photos" on page 120 to learn how to recover deleted photos within 30 days of deleting them.

8. Creating a Photo Album

You can create a photo album right on your iPad. To create a photo album:

1. Touch the ![icon] icon. The Photos application opens.
2. Touch **Albums** at the bottom of the screen. A list of photo albums appears.
3. Touch the ![plus] button at the top of the screen. The New Album window appears, as shown in **Figure 5**.
4. Enter a name for the album and touch **Save**. The new photo album is created, and you can now choose photos to add to it.
5. Touch a photo album, and then touch the photos that you want to add. Touch a photo a second time to deselect it. Touch **Albums** at the bottom of the screen at any time to return to the album list.
6. Touch **Done** at the top of the screen. The selected photos are added to the new photo album.

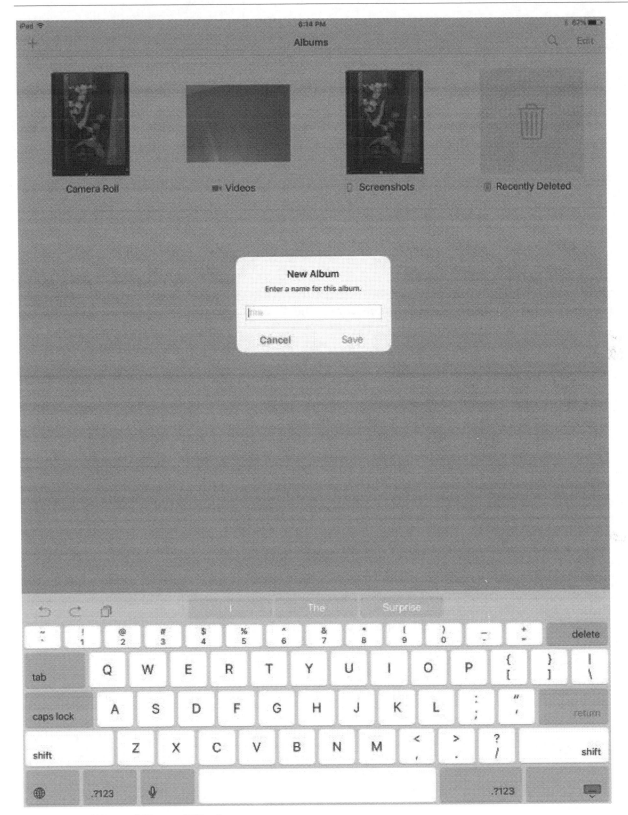

Figure 5: New Album Window

9. Editing a Photo Album

Photo albums stored on the iPad can be edited right from your iPad. Refer to *"Creating a Photo Album"* on page 110 to learn how to make a new photo album using your iPad.

To edit the name of a photo album:

1. Touch the ![icon] icon. The Photos application opens.
2. Touch **Albums** at the bottom of the screen. A list of photo albums appears.

3. Touch **Edit** at the top of the screen. The ![button] button appears next to each album that may be edited.
4. Touch the name of a photo album. The virtual keyboard appears.
5. Enter a new name for the album and touch **Done**. The album is renamed.

Note: Any album that is grayed out after you touch 'Edit' cannot be deleted or renamed.
To add photos to an album:

1. Touch the ![icon] icon. The Photos application opens.
2. Touch **Albums** at the bottom of the screen. A list of photo albums appears.
3. Touch an album. The photos contained in the album appear.
4. Touch **Select** in the upper right-hand corner of the screen. Photos can now be selected.
5. Touch as many photos as desired. The ![icon] icons appear on the selected photos, as shown in **Figure 6**.
6. Touch **Add To**. A list of photo albums appears. You cannot add photos to any album that is grayed out.
7. Touch the name of a photo album. The selected photos are added to the album.

Note: Adding photos to an album does not remove them from the original album.

Figure 6: Selected Photos

10. Deleting a Photo Album

Photo albums stored on the iPad can be deleted right from your iPad. To delete a photo album:

Warning: When an album is deleted from the iPad, any photos that are stored in other albums will remain on the iPad. Make sure any photos you wish to keep are stored in another album. Refer to "Editing a Photo Album" on page 112 to learn how to add photos to an album.

1. Touch the ⬛ icon. The Photos application opens.
2. Touch **Albums** at the bottom of the screen. A list of photo albums appears.
3. Touch **Edit** at the top of the screen. The ⓧ button appears next to each album that may be deleted.
4. Touch the ⓧ button next to an album. 'Delete' appears.
5. Touch **Delete**. The photo album is deleted.

11. Starting a Slideshow

The iPad can play a slideshow using the photos in your albums. To begin a slideshow:

1. Touch the ⬛ icon. The Photos application opens.
2. Touch **Albums** at the bottom of the screen. A list of photo albums appears.
3. Touch an album. The photos in the album appear.
4. Touch **Slideshow** at the top of the screen. The slideshow begins.
5. Touch anywhere on the screen, and then touch **Options**. The Slideshow Settings window appears, as shown in **Figure 7**.
6. Touch **Theme** and select the transition for the slideshow. You may also touch **Music**, and then touch **iTunes Music** to select the Music from your library.

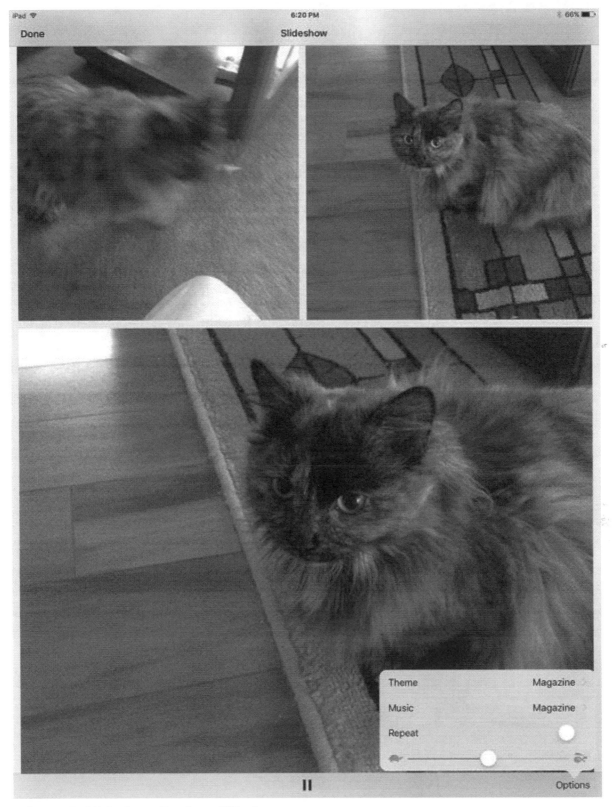

Figure 7: Slideshow Settings Window

12. Browsing Photos by Date and Location

The iPad can sort photos according to the physical locations where they were taken, as well as the dates on which they were captured. To browse photos by date and location:

1. Touch the ![icon] icon. The Photos application opens.
2. Touch **Photos** at the bottom of the screen. The Moments screen appears.
3. Touch **Collections** at the top of the screen. A list of albums appears, organized by date and location, as shown in **Figure 8**.
4. Touch an album in any location. The selected album opens.
5. Touch the name of a town. A map appears, showing the locations where photos were taken. Touch **Collections** to return to the photo list.

Note: You may only view pictures sorted by location if you have Location Services turned on. Refer to "Turning Location Services On or Off" *on page 206 to learn more.*

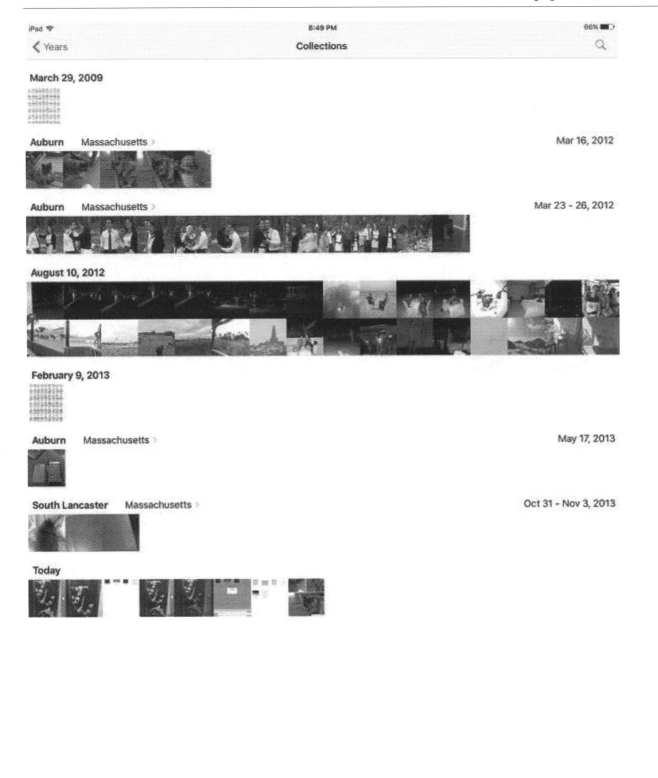

Figure 8: List of Albums Organized by Date and Location

13. Searching for a Photo

Use the Search feature to find a photo more quickly while viewing the Photos application. To search for a photo:

1. Touch the $\mathcal{Q}$ icon at the top of the screen while using the Photos application. 'Search Photos' appears.
2. Enter the name of the album, or the location where the photo was taken. You may also search by date.
3. Touch **Search**. A list of matching results appears as you type, as shown in **Figure 9**.

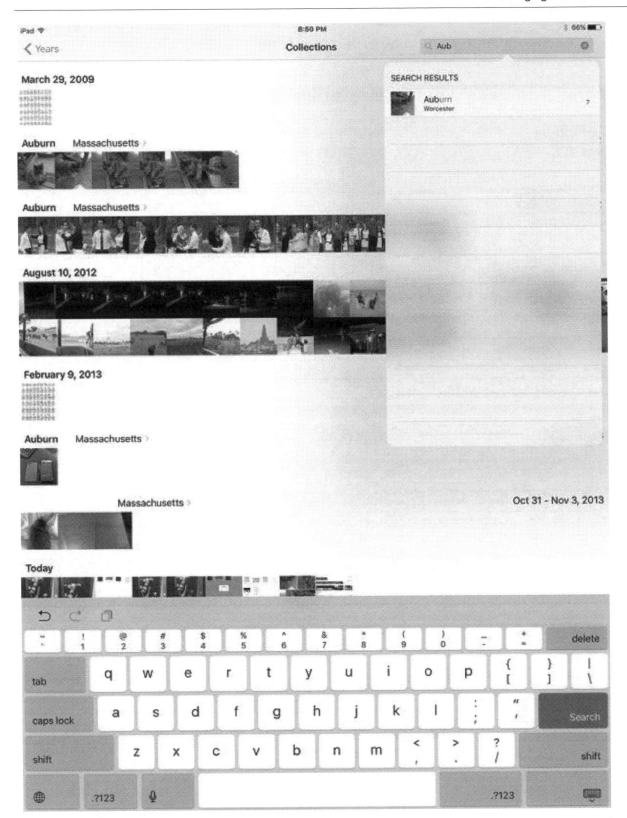

Figure 9: List of Matching Photo Results

14. Recording a Time-Lapse Video

You can record a time-lapse video, which allows you to capture a short video of an event that takes place over a long period of time, such as the budding of a flower. To record a time-lapse video:

1. Touch the icon. The camera turns on.
2. Touch **Time-Lapse**. The time-lapse camcorder turns on.
3. Touch the button. The camcorder begins to record the time-lapse video.
4. Touch the button. The time-lapse video is captured and stored in the 'Time-lapse' album. The Photos application marks every time-lapse video with the icon.

15. Recovering Deleted Photos

You may recover a deleted photo if fewer than 30 days have passed since you deleted it. To recover deleted photos:

1. Touch the icon. The Photos application opens.
2. Touch **Albums** at the bottom of the screen. A list of photo albums appears.
3. Touch the **Recently Deleted** album. The recently deleted photos appear. The number of days on each photo shows the amount of time left before the photo will be permanently deleted.
4. Touch **Select** at the top of the screen, and then touch each photo that you want to recover. The icons appear on the selected photos.
5. Touch **Recover** at the top of the screen. The selected photos are returned to their original albums.

Using iTunes on the iPad

Table of Contents

1. Registering with Apple

In order to buy content, you will need to have an iTunes account. Refer to *"Signing In to an iTunes Account"* on page 169 to learn more.

2. Buying Music and Ringtones in iTunes

Music and ringtones can be purchased directly from the iPad via iTunes. To buy music using the iTunes application:

1. Touch the ![icon] icon. The iTunes application opens.
2. Touch the ![icon] icon. The iTunes Music Store opens and the new releases are shown.
3. Touch **Genres** at the top of the screen to browse music. A list of Genres appears. You may also search for a specific song or artist by touching **Search**.
4. Touch an album. The Album description appears, as shown in **Figure 1**.
5. Touch the price of the album. 'Buy Album' appears.
6. Touch **Buy Album** or **Pre-Order Album** (if the album has not yet been released). The album is purchased. Touch the price of a song and then touch **Buy Song** to buy a single song.
7. To purchase a ringtone, follow steps 1-3, and then touch the name of the ringtone. Touch **Buy** to purchase the ringtone.

Note: You may need to enter your iTunes password when purchasing music on the iPad.

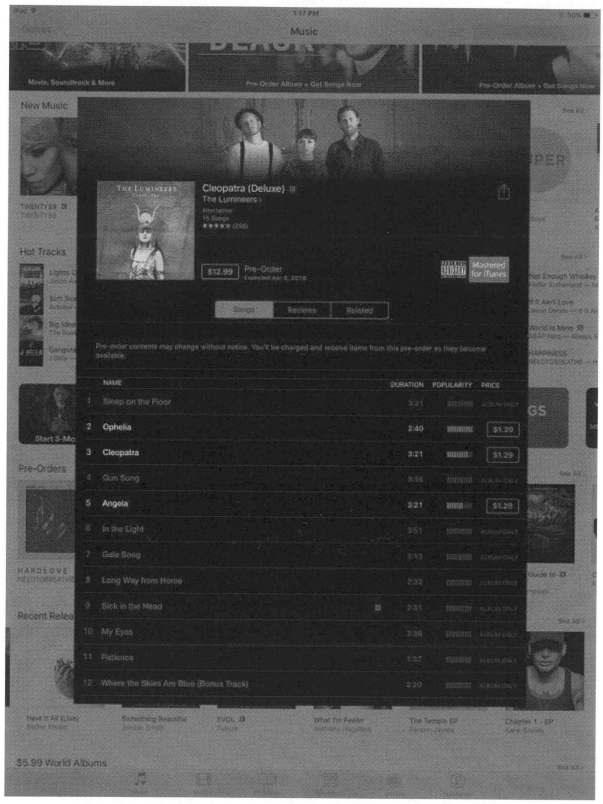

Figure 1: Album Description

3. Buying or Renting Videos in iTunes

Videos can be purchased or rented directly from the iPad and viewed using the Music application. To buy videos using the iTunes application:

1. Touch the ⊙ icon. The iTunes application opens.
2. Touch the ▦ icon or the ▦ icon. The iTunes Video Store opens, and the featured videos appear, as shown in **Figure 2** (Movie Store).
3. Touch **Genres** at the top of the screen to browse videos.
4. Touch a video. The Video description appears, as shown in **Figure 3**.
5. Touch the price of the video. 'Buy Movie' (or 'Buy HD Movie'), 'Rent Movie', or 'Buy HD Episode' appears, depending on your selection.
6. Touch **Buy NAME**, where NAME refers to the type of video that you are buying. The iPad may ask for your iTunes password. The video is purchased or rented, and the download begins.

Note: When renting a video, the video is available for 24 hours once you start watching it. Once 24 hours has passed, you will not be able to resume the video if you pause it.

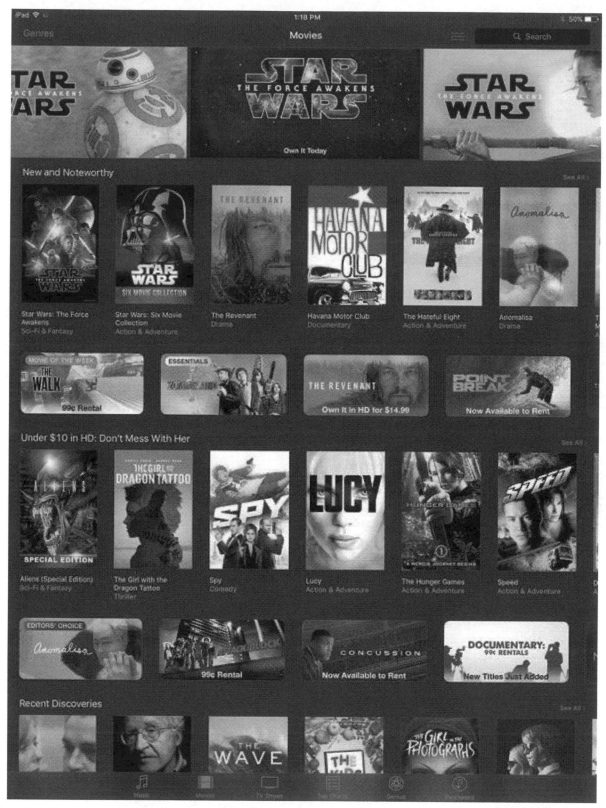

Figure 2: iTunes Video Store (Movies)

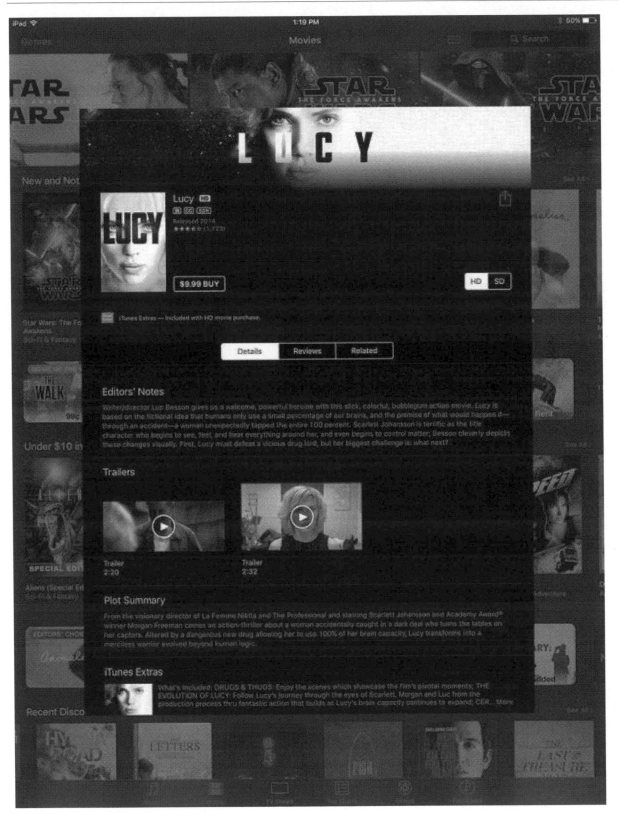

Figure 3: Video Description

4. Searching for Media in iTunes

The iPad can search for any media in the iTunes Store. To search for media:

1. Touch the ⬚ icon. The iTunes application opens.
2. Touch the ⬚ icon. 'Search' appears at the top of the screen. Touch the ⬚ button to clear the field, if necessary.
3. Enter the name of an artist, actor, song, or video that you wish to find. Touch **Search**. The matching results appear, organized by the type of media, as shown in **Figure 4**.
4. Touch a song, video, or ringtone. The media description appears.

Note: Refer to "Buying Music and Ringtones in iTunes" *on page 121 or* "Buying or Renting Videos in iTunes" *on page 123 to learn how to purchase media.*

Figure 4: Available Media Results

5. Playing Media

To play media purchased in iTunes on the iPad, use the Music Application. To learn how, refer to *"Using the Music Application"* on page 131.

6. Sharing Your iTunes Account with Family

You may allow your friends or family members to purchase content using your iTunes account. Make sure that you trust the people to whom you give access to your iTunes account. To share your iTunes account:

1. Touch the icon. The Settings screen appears, as shown in **Figure 5**.
2. Scroll down and touch **iCloud**. The iCloud Settings appear, as shown in **Figure 6**.
3. Touch **Set Up Family Sharing**. The Family Sharing window appears.
4. Touch **Get Started**. The Family Setup begins.
5. Touch **Continue**. The Purchase Sharing screen appears.
6. Touch **Continue**. The Terms and Conditions appear.
7. Touch **Agree**, and then touch **Agree** again. The Payment Method screen appears.
8. Confirm that your payment method is correct, and touch **Continue**. The Location Sharing screen appears.
9. Touch **Share Your Location** to allow your family members or friends to view your location at all times, or touch **Not Now** to keep your location private. The Family settings appear.
10. Touch **Add Family Member**. The Add Family Member dialog appears.
11. Enter the name or email address of the family member or friend, and touch **Next**. An invitation to use your iTunes account is sent, and your contact may now use your account.

Figure 5: Settings Screen

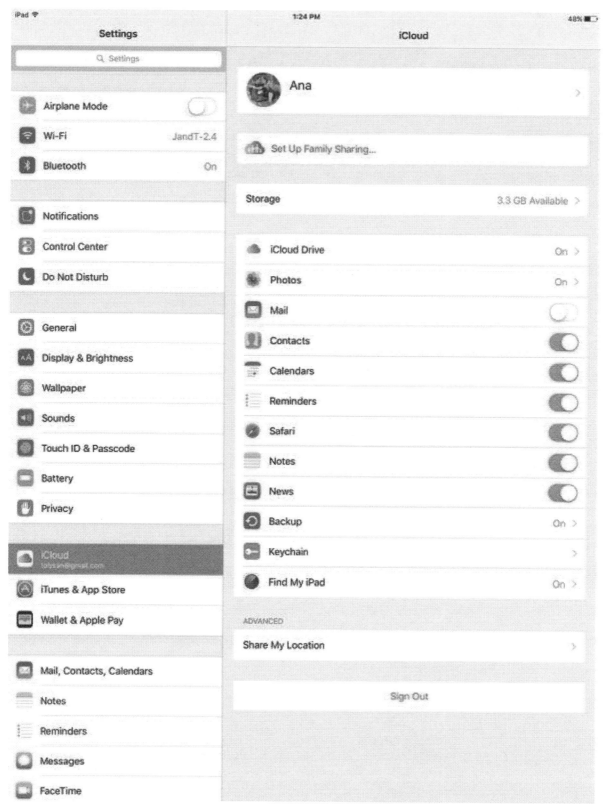

Figure 6: iCloud Settings

Using the Music Application

Table of Contents

1. Downloading Media

Use the iTunes Application to download media to the iPad. Refer to *"Using iTunes on the iPad"* on page 121 to learn how.

2. Playing Music

The Music application on the iPad can be used to play music. To listen to your music:

1. Touch the icon. The Music application opens.
2. Touch one of the following icons at the bottom of the screen to browse music:

 - Browse existing playlists.

 - Browse existing artists.

♩ - Browse existing songs.

3. Use the following tips to navigate the Music Application:
   - Touch a playlist, artist, or song to play the item. The item plays, as shown in **Figure 1**.
   - After you have exited the Music application, touch the screen at the bottom and drag your finger up to bring up the music controls, as shown in **Figure 2**.
   - Touch the name of the artist to return to the Music application.
     The music controls will also appear on the lock screen, as shown in **Figure 3**.

Figure 1: Music Playing

Figure 2: Music Controls

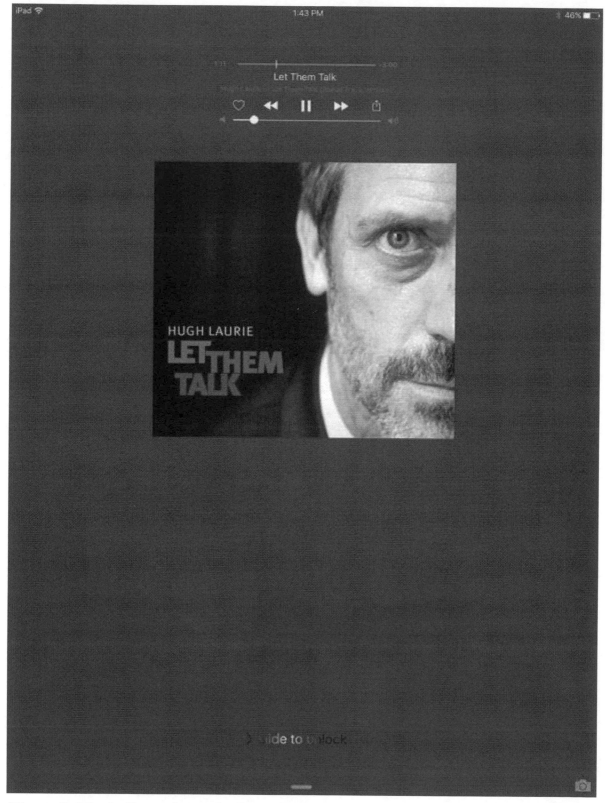

Figure 3: Music Controls on the Lock Screen

3. Using Additional Audio Controls

Use the Song Controls to control music while it is playing. Touch one of the following to perform the corresponding function:

◀◀ - Skip to the beginning of the current song or skip to the previous song.

▶▶ - Skip to the next song.

❚❚ - Pause the current song.

▶ - Resume the current song when it is paused.

≡ - View the current playlist.

⟲ - Repeat the song or artist that is currently playing.

────────── - Drag the ❘ on the bar below the album art to go to a different part of the song.

⤩ - Shuffle all songs in the playlist. Touch again to play the songs in order.

Create - Create an iTunes Radio station from the artist or song that is currently playing.

*Note: Touch both **Repeat** and **Shuffle** to play songs continuously in random order. To shuffle and play all songs on the iPad, go to the song list and touch **Shuffle**.*

4. Creating a Playlist

Playlists can be created in iTunes. However, the Music application can perform the same function. To create a playlist in the Music application:

1. Touch the 🎵 icon in the Music application. The existing playlists appear.
2. Touch **New Playlist**. The New Playlist screen appears, as shown in **Figure 4**.
3. Enter the name of the playlist and touch **Add Songs**. A list of music categories on your iPad appears, as shown in **Figure 5**.
4. Touch one of the categories to browse music to add to the new playlist.
5. Touch a song. A check mark appears next to each song that is added to the playlist.
6. Touch **Done**. The playlist is populated with the selected music.
7. Touch **Done**. The playlist is saved.

After creating a playlist, you can add or remove music from it. To edit a playlist:

1. Touch **Playlists** in the Music application. The existing playlists appear.
2. Touch a playlist. The Playlist screen appears, as shown in **Figure 6**.
3. Touch **Edit**. A ⊖ button appears next to every song in the playlist.
4. Touch the ⊖ button next to a song, and touch **Delete**. The song is removed from the playlist.
5. To add songs, touch **Add Songs**, and then repeat steps 4 and 5 from the instructions above. The selected songs are added to the playlist.
6. Touch **Done**. The changes to the playlist are saved.

Note: Removing a song from a playlist will not delete it from the Music library.

Figure 4: New Playlist Window

iPad 🤖	1:47 PM	⚹ 45% 🔋
	Add Music	Done

Q Search Music

🎤 Artists   >

🎵 Albums   >

♪ Songs   >

🎬 Music Videos   >

Genres   >

Composers   >

Playlists   >

Figure 5: List of Music Categories

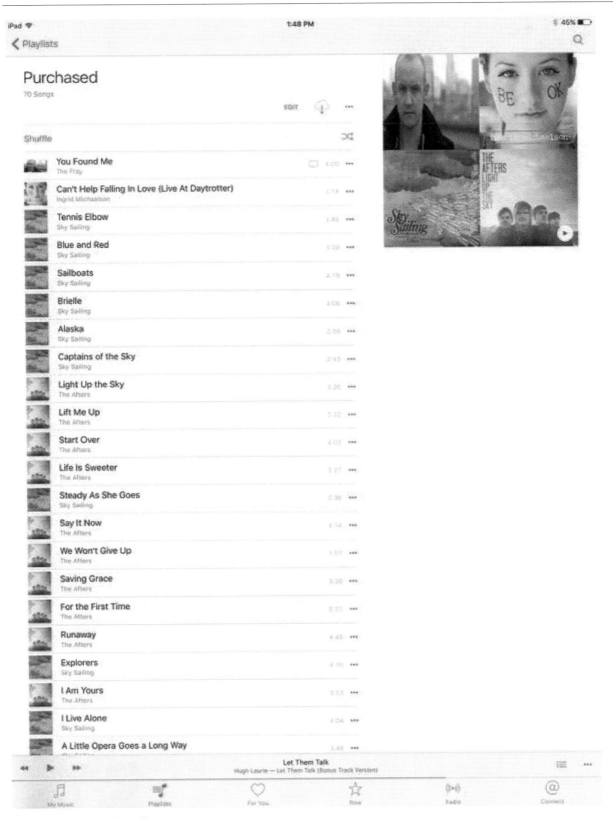

Figure 6: Playlist Screen

5. Using the iTunes Radio

The iTunes Radio is a free service that allows you to create personalized stations based on artists, songs, or genres.

To create a new iTunes Radio station, touch the ((•)) icon in the Music application. The iTunes Radio screen appears, as shown in **Figure 7**. Touch a genre in the list, or touch the search field at the top of the screen, and enter an artist, genre, or song. If you search for a station, touch the name of the artist, album, or song. The station begins to play, and is added to your list of stations automatically.

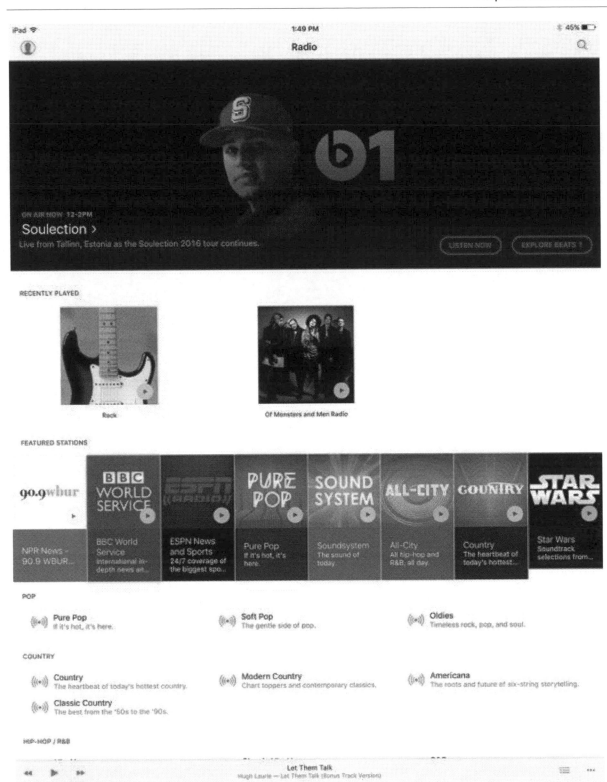

Figure 7: iTunes Radio Screen

Using the Mail Application

Table of Contents

1. Setting Up the Mail Application

Before the Email application can be used, at least one account must be set up on your iPad. To set up the Email application:

1. Touch the icon. The Settings screen appears, as shown in **Figure 1**.
2. Scroll down and touch **Mail, Contacts, Calendars**. The Mail, Contacts, Calendars screen appears, as shown in **Figure 2**.
3. Touch **Add Account**. The Account Type screen appears, as shown in **Figure 3**.
4. Touch one of the email services in the list to set up an email account. The corresponding email setup screen appears.
5. Enter all of the required information, and touch **Next** at the top of the screen. The email account is added to your iPad.

Figure 1: Settings Screen

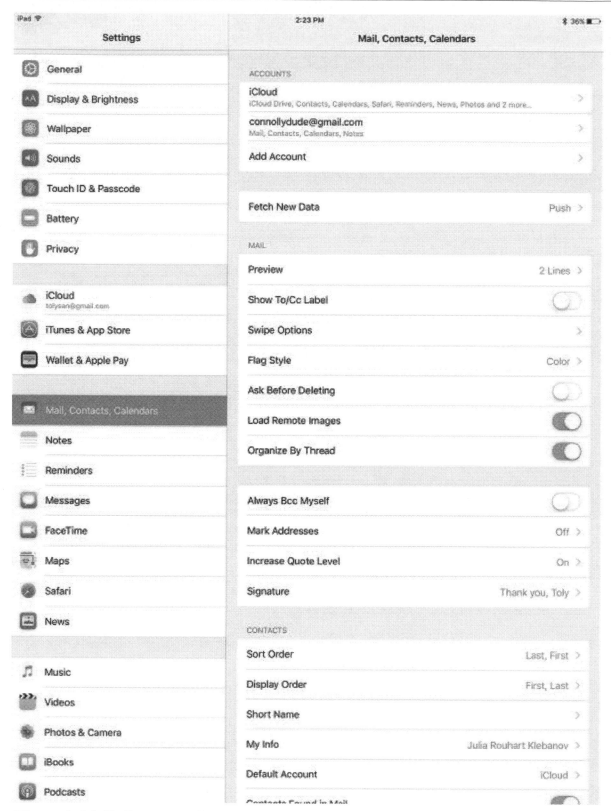

Figure 2: Mail, Contacts, Calendars Screen

iPad 🔋	4:53 PM	⚹ 28% ▭
Settings	‹ Mail, Contacts... **Add Account**	

🔍 Settings

✈ Airplane Mode	⬭	
📶 Wi-Fi	JandT-2.4	
ⓑ Bluetooth	On	

📵 Notifications

🎛 Control Center

🌙 Do Not Disturb

⚙ General

🔆 Display & Brightness

✿ Wallpaper

🔊 Sounds

☝ Touch ID & Passcode

🔋 Battery

✋ Privacy

☁ iCloud
tolysan@gmail.com

Ⓐ iTunes & App Store

💳 Wallet & Apple Pay

✉ Mail, Contacts, Calendars

📝 Notes

☰ Reminders

💬 Messages

📷 FaceTime

☁ iCloud

E⊠ Exchange

Google

YAHOO!

Aol.

O⊠ Outlook.com

Other

Figure 3: Account Type Screen

2. Reading Email

You can read your email on the iPad via the Email application. Before opening the Email application, make sure you have set up your email account. Refer to *"Setting Up the Email Application"* on page 142 to learn how. To read your email:

1. Touch the ![envelope icon] icon. The Email application opens and the Inbox appears, as shown in **Figure 4**. If the emails are not shown, touch **Inbox** at the top of the screen.
2. Touch an email. The email opens.
3. Touch **Inbox** at the top of the screen in an email to return to the list of received emails. Touch **Mailboxes** at the top of the Inbox to return to the list of mailboxes. The mailbox list varies depending on the mail service.

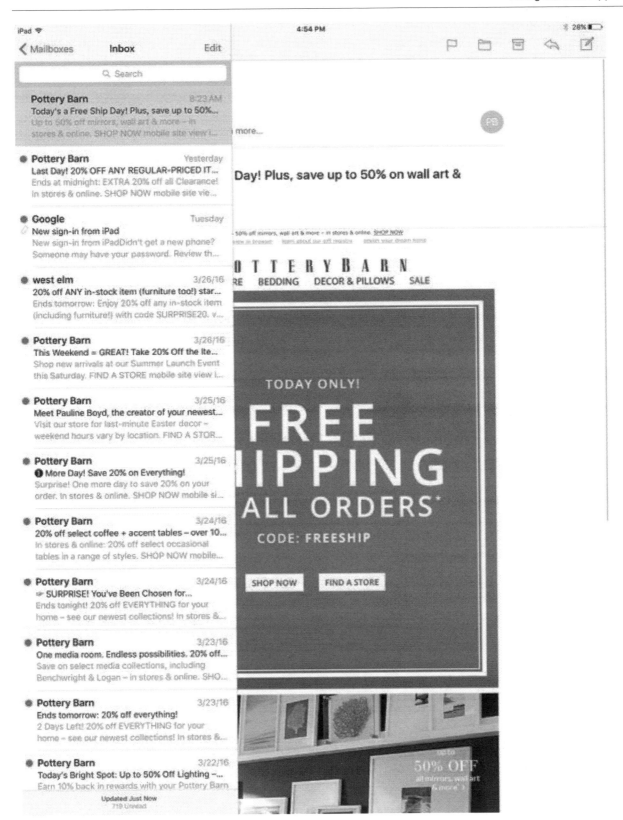

Figure 4: Email Inbox

3. Switching Accounts in the Email Application

If you have more than one active email account, you can switch between them, or view all of your email in one Inbox. To switch to another account:

1. Touch the icon. The Email application opens and your emails appear.
2. Touch **Mailboxes** at the top of the screen while viewing a list of messages in a folder. A list of all active inboxes and accounts appears, as shown in **Figure 5**.
3. Touch an account. The Inbox associated with the selected account appears.

You can also touch **All Inboxes** to view all emails from the accounts attached to your iPad in a single joint folder.

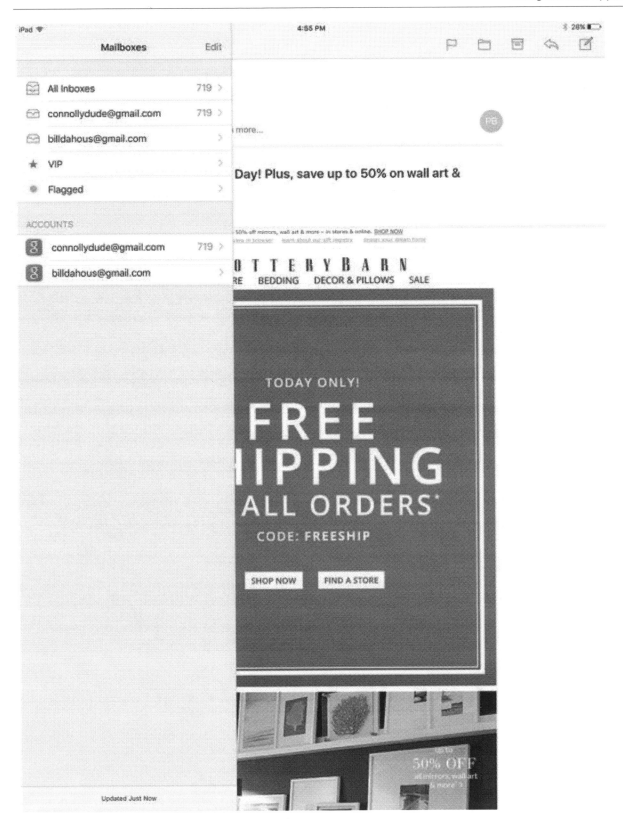

Figure 5: List of Active Inboxes and Accounts

4. Writing an Email

Compose email directly from the iPad using the Email application. To write an email while using the Email application:

1. Touch the ✏️ button. The New Email screen appears, as shown in **Figure 6**.
2. Start entering the name of a contact. A list of matching contacts appears as you type.
3. Touch the name of the contact that you wish to email. The contact's email address is added to the addressee list. Alternatively, enter an email address from scratch. Enter as many additional addressees as desired.
4. Touch the **return** key on the keyboard. The cursor jumps to the subject of the email. Enter a topic for the message.
5. Touch the **return** key on the keyboard. The cursor jumps to the body of the email. Enter the content of the email, and touch **Send** at the top of the screen. The email is sent.

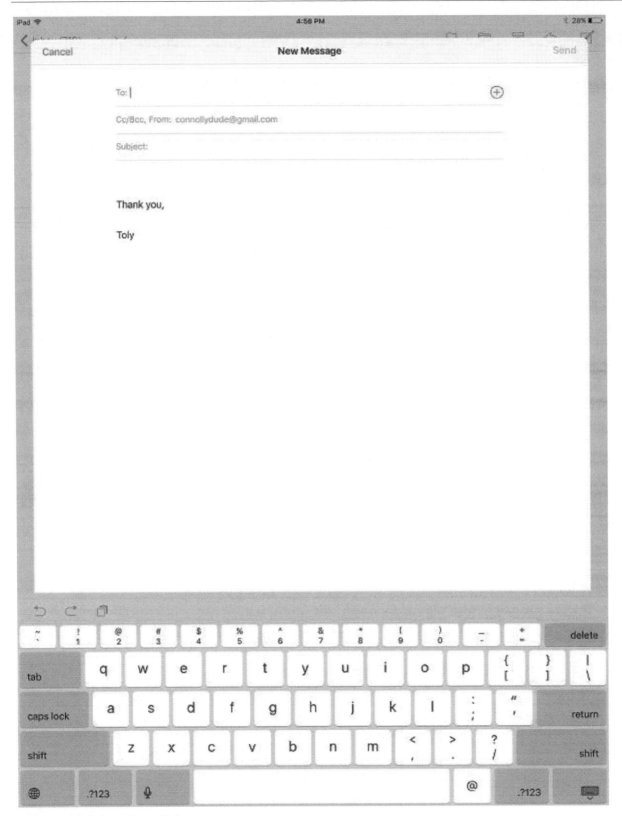

Figure 6: New Email Screen

5. Referring to Another Email when Composing a New Message

While composing an email, you may wish to refer to another message for reference. To do so, touch and hold **New Message** at the top of the screen, and drag your finger to the bottom of the screen. The New Message screen is hidden, and you may use the Email application normally. To continue writing your email where you left off, touch **New Message** at the bottom of the screen. If you have already entered a subject, 'New Message' will be replaced by the subject.

6. Formatting Text

When writing an email on your iPad, you can format the text to add bold, italics, underline, or increase the quote level.

To add bold, italics, or underline text while writing an email:

1. Touch and hold the text in the email that you wish to format. The Select menu appears above the text, as shown in **Figure 7**.
2. Touch **Select All**. All of the text is selected. To select a single word, touch **Select**. Blue dots appear around the word or phrase.
3. Touch and hold one of the blue dots and drag it in any direction. The text between the dots is highlighted and a Text menu appears, as shown in **Figure 8**.
4. Touch the button. 'Bold', 'Italics', and 'Underline' appear. If you do not see button, touch the button in the Text menu.
5. Touch one of the formatting options. The associated formatting is applied to the selected text.

You can also increase the left margin, or quote level, in an email. To increase the quote level:

1. Touch and hold any location in your email. The text cursor flashes in the selected location.
2. Touch the button in the Text menu. The Text Format menu appears. If you are using an iPad, proceed to step 3.
3. Touch **Quote Level**. The Quote Level options appear.
4. Touch **Decrease** or **Increase** to adjust the Quote Level accordingly. The new Quote Level is set and applied to the paragraph where the text cursor is currently flashing.

Figure 7: Select Menu

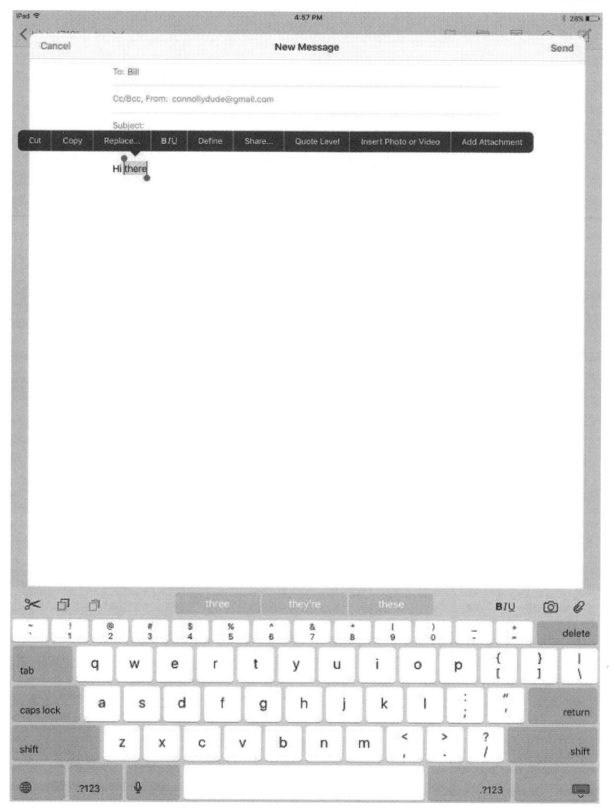

Figure 8: Text Menu

7. Replying to and Forwarding Email Messages

After receiving an email, you can reply to the sender or forward the email to a new recipient. To reply to, or forward, an email message:

1. Touch the ▨ icon. The Email application opens.
2. Touch an email. The email appears.
3. Touch the ↰ button. The Reply menu appears, as shown in **Figure 9**.
4. Touch **Reply** to reply to the message, or touch **Forward** to forward the message. The New Message screen appears. The subject at the top is preceded by 'Re:' if replying or 'Fwd:' if forwarding. The original email is copied in the body. If replying, the addressee field is filled in.
5. Touch the text field next to 'To:', and enter an addressee, if necessary. The addressee is entered. The address of the sender is automatically entered when replying to an email.
6. Touch the text field to the right of 'Subject' to enter a different subject for your message, if desired. The subject is entered.
7. Touch the text field below 'Subject' and enter a message, if desired. The message is entered.
8. Touch **Send** at the top of the screen. The email is sent.

*Note: When forwarding an email, the attachment menu will appear if the original message has an attachment. Touch **Include** if you wish to include the attachment when you forward the email. Otherwise, touch **Don't Include**.*

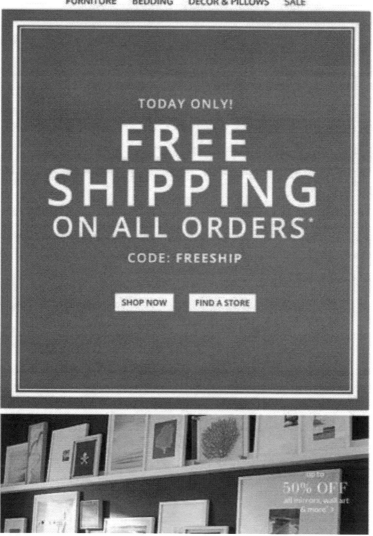

Figure 9: Reply Menu

8. Attaching a Picture or Video to an Email

While composing an email, you may wish to attach a picture or video to send to the recipient. To attach a picture or video to an email:

1. Touch the 📷 icon above the keyboard, as outlined in **Figure 10**. A list of photo albums stored on your iPad appears, as shown in **Figure 10**.
2. Touch the photo album that contains the photo that you wish to attach. The photo album opens and a list of photo thumbnails appears, as shown in **Figure 11**.
3. Touch the photo that you wish to attach. A preview of the photo appears.
4. Touch **Use**. The selected photo is attached. Alternatively, touch **Cancel** to return to the list of photos. You can always delete the photo from the email by touching **delete** on the keyboard.

Note: You may move or delete the photo in the same way that you would delete text.

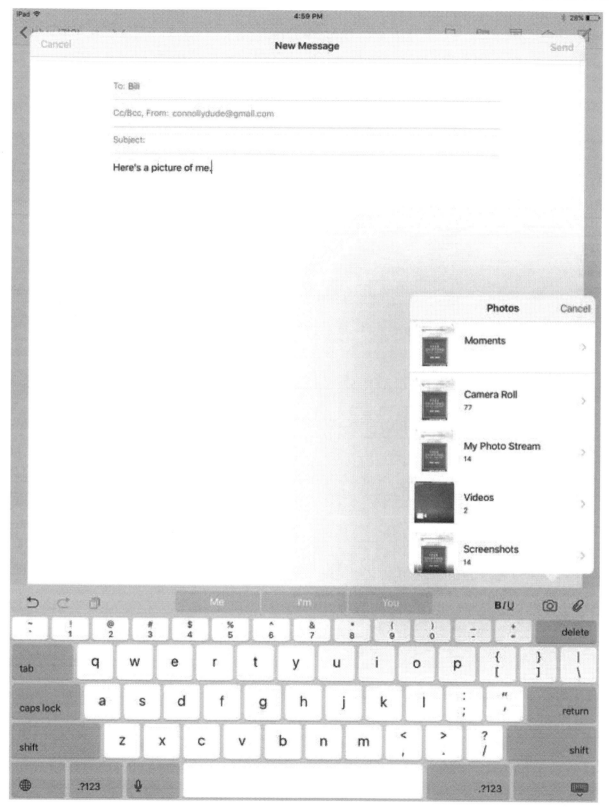

Figure 10: List of Photo Albums

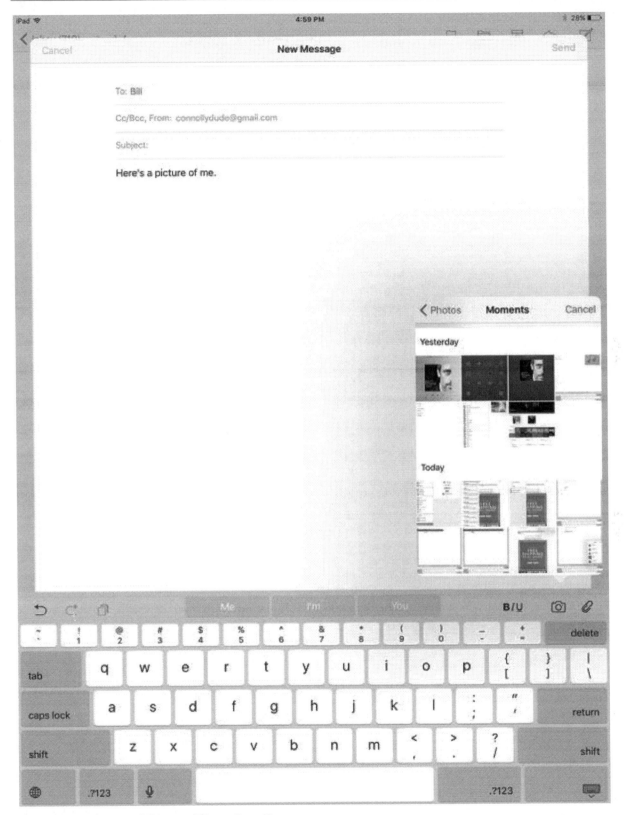

Figure 11: List of Photo Thumbnails

9. Moving an Email in the Inbox to Another Folder

You may wish to organize emails into folders so that you can find them more easily. To move an email in the Inbox to another folder:

1. Touch an email in the Inbox. The email opens.
2. Touch the button at the top of the screen. A list of available folders appears, as shown in **Figure 12**.
3. Touch the name of a folder. The selected email is moved to the selected folder. To view a list of your folders, touch **Mailboxes** at the top of the screen while viewing the Inbox.

Figure 12: List of Available Folders

10. Flagging an Important Email

You may flag emails that are of the greatest importance in order to find them more quickly. This feature is especially useful if you do not have the time to read the email immediately, and wish to return to it in the near future. To flag an important email:

1. Touch an email in the Inbox. The email opens.

2. Touch the [flag icon] button at the top of the screen. The Flagging menu appears, as shown in **Figure 13**.

3. Touch **Flag**. The email is flagged as 'Important'. You may also touch **Mark as Unread** to flag the email so that you remember to read it later.

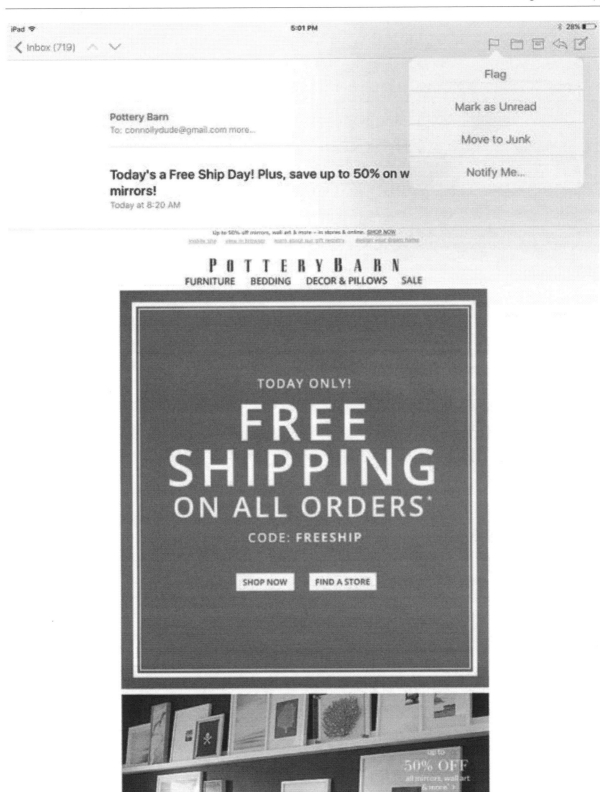

Figure 13: Flagging Menu

11. Archiving Emails

You may archive emails from your Inbox to free up space and improve organization. Archiving emails moves them to a folder that does not take up space on your iPad. Therefore, you never need to delete an email, and can always recover it if you did not mean to delete it. You may archive as many emails as you like. To archive an email:

1. Touch the ![envelope icon] icon. The email application opens.
2. Touch and hold an email in the list and drag your finger to the left until the email disappears. The email is sent to the 'All Mail' folder, and disappears from the Inbox. You can also archive an email by touching the ![archive icon] icon at the top of the screen while viewing an open email.
3. Touch **Mailboxes** at the top of the screen, and then touch **All Mail** to view all emails, including those that have been archived.

12. Changing the Default Signature

The iPad can set a default signature that will be attached to the end of each email that is sent from the iPad. To set or change this signature:

1. Touch the ![settings icon] icon. The Settings screen appears.
2. Touch **Mail, Contacts, Calendars**. The Mail, Contacts, Calendars screen appears.
3. Touch **Signature**. The Signature screen appears, as shown in **Figure 14**.
4. If you have more than one account registered on your iPad, touch **All Accounts** to assign the same signature to each account. Otherwise, touch **Per Account**, and touch the signature under the account that you want to edit.
5. Enter a signature, and then touch **Mail, Contacts** at the top of the screen. The new signature is saved.

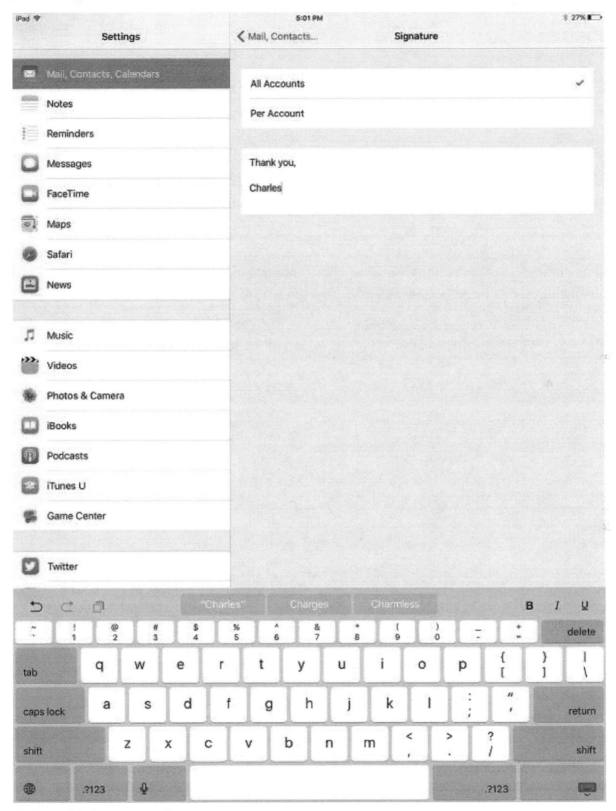

Figure 14: Signature Screen

13. Changing How You Receive Email

There are two options for receiving email on the iPad. The iPad can check for new email only when you refresh the Inbox, or it can constantly check for email and display an alert when a new email arrives. To set the iPad to either check for email at regular intervals or only when you refresh the Inbox:

1. Touch the ⚙ icon. The Settings screen appears.
2. Touch **Mail, Contacts, Calendars** at the bottom of the screen. The Mail, Contacts, Calendars screen appears.
3. Touch **Fetch New Data**. The Fetch New Data screen appears, as shown in **Figure 15**.

4. Touch the ⬭ switch next to 'Push'. Push is turned on, and the Email application will constantly check for new email and alert you when a new one arrives.

5. Touch the ⬬ switch next to 'Push'. Push is turned off, and the Email application will only check for new email when you touch the top of the Inbox and slide your finger down to refresh it.

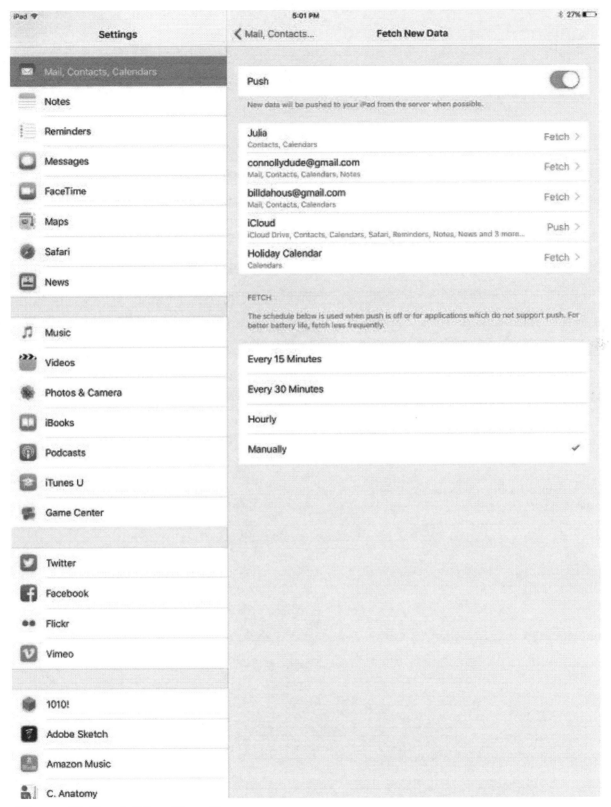

Figure 15: Fetch New Data Screen

14. Changing Email Options

There are various options that change the way your Email application works. Touch the icon, and then touch **Mail, Contacts, Calendars** to change one of the following options:

- **Preview** - Choose the number of lines of an email message to preview in the Inbox.

- **Show To/Cc Label** - Choose whether to hide the 'To' and 'Cc' labels and show only addresses.

- **Swipe Options** - Changes the swipe action used to flag an email, or mark an email as 'Unread'.

- **Flag Style** - Choose the type of shape to use (color or shape) when flagging an email.

- **Ask Before Deleting** - Choose whether to display a confirmation before deleting an email.

- **Load Remote Images** - Choose whether to load images in an email automatically.

- **Organize by Thread** - Choose whether to group all emails with the same contact as a conversation.

- **Always Bcc Myself** - Choose whether the email application sends a copy of each email to your own email address for your records.

- **Increase Quote Level -** Choose whether to increase the left margin when replying to or forwarding an email.

- **Default Account** - Choose which account appears by default when you open the Email application.

Managing Applications

Table of Contents

1. Signing In to an iTunes Account

In order to buy applications, you will need to have an iTunes account. To set up a new iTunes account:

1. Touch the icon. The Settings screen appears, as shown in **Figure 1**.
2. Scroll down and touch **iTunes & App Store**. The iTunes & App Store Settings screen appears, as shown in **Figure 2**.
3. If you already have an Apple ID, touch **Sign In** and enter your Apple ID and password. Otherwise, touch **Create New Apple ID** to register for an Apple ID.

Figure 1: Settings Screen

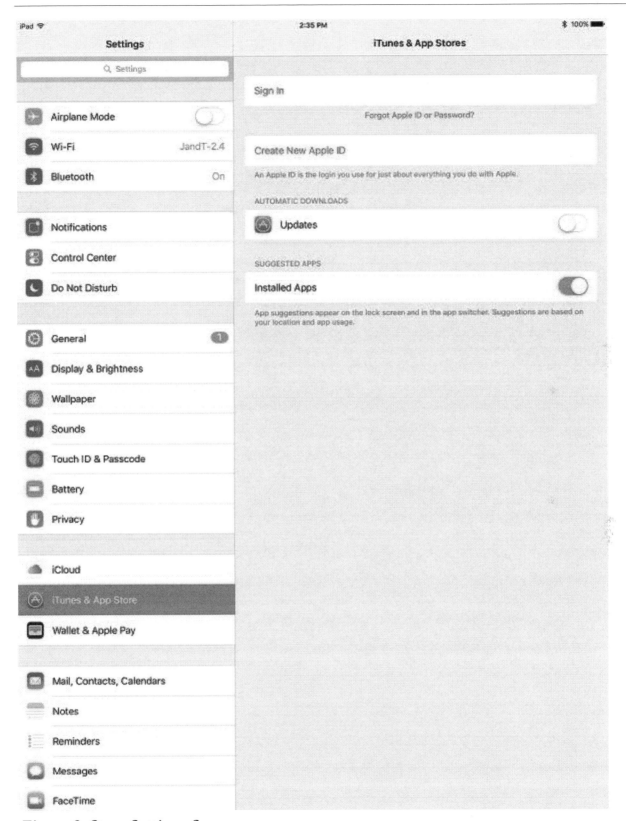

Figure 2: Store Settings Screen

2. Signing In to a Different iTunes Account

If more than one person uses your iPad, you may wish to sign in with an alternate Apple ID. Only one Apple ID may be signed in at a time. To sign out and sign in to a different iTunes account:

1. Touch the ⚙ icon. The Settings screen appears.
2. Scroll down and touch **iTunes & App Store**. The iTunes & App Store Settings screen appears. If someone is signed in to their iTunes account on the iPad, their email appears at the top of the screen.
3. Touch the email address at the top of the screen. The Apple ID window appears, as shown in **Figure 3**.
4. Touch **Sign Out**. The account is signed out.
5. Touch **Sign In**. The Sign In window appears.
6. Enter your registered email address and password.
7. Touch **Sign In**. The account is signed in, and the owner's email is shown at the top of the iTunes & App Store screen.

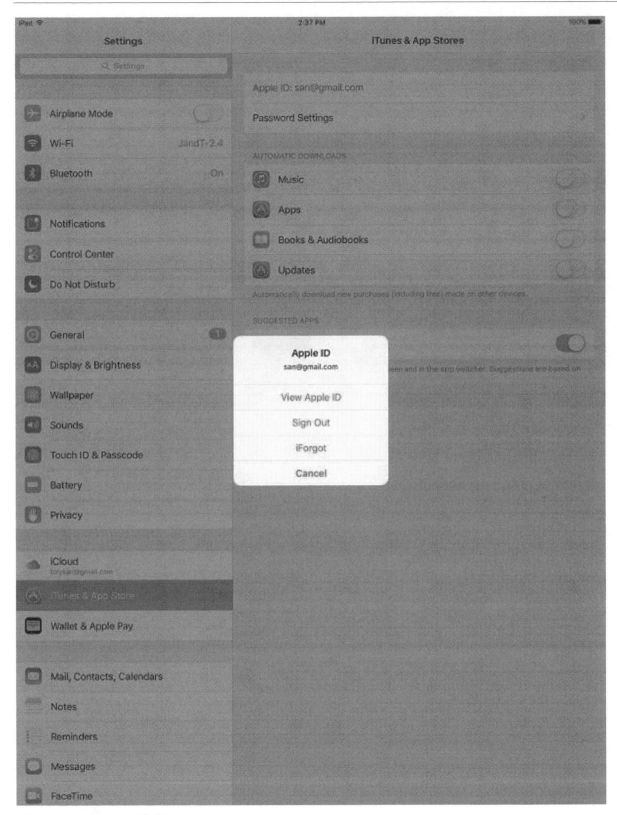

Figure 3: Apple ID Window

3. Editing iTunes Account Information

You must keep your account information up to date in order to purchase applications from the iTunes Application Store. For instance, when your billing address changes or your credit card expires, you must change your information. To edit iTunes account information:

1. Touch the ⬤ icon. The Settings screen appears.
2. Scroll down and touch **iTunes & App Store**. The iTunes & App Store Settings screen appears. If someone is signed in to their iTunes account on the iPad, their email appears at the top of the screen.
3. If you are not already signed in, enter your registered email and password, and touch **Done**. You are signed in.
4. Touch your email at the top of the screen. The Apple ID window appears.
5. Touch **View Apple ID**. The Account Screen appears with your personal account information.
6. Touch a field to edit it, and then touch **Done**. The new information is saved.

4. Searching for an Application to Purchase

Use the Application Store to search for applications. There are three ways to search for applications:

Manual Search

To search for an application manually:

1. Touch the ⬤ icon. The Application Store opens, as shown in **Figure 4**.
2. Touch the 🔍 button. The Search field appears at the top of the screen.
3. Touch **Search**. The virtual keyboard appears at the bottom of the screen.
4. Enter the name of an application and touch **Search** at the bottom of the screen. A list of matching results appears.

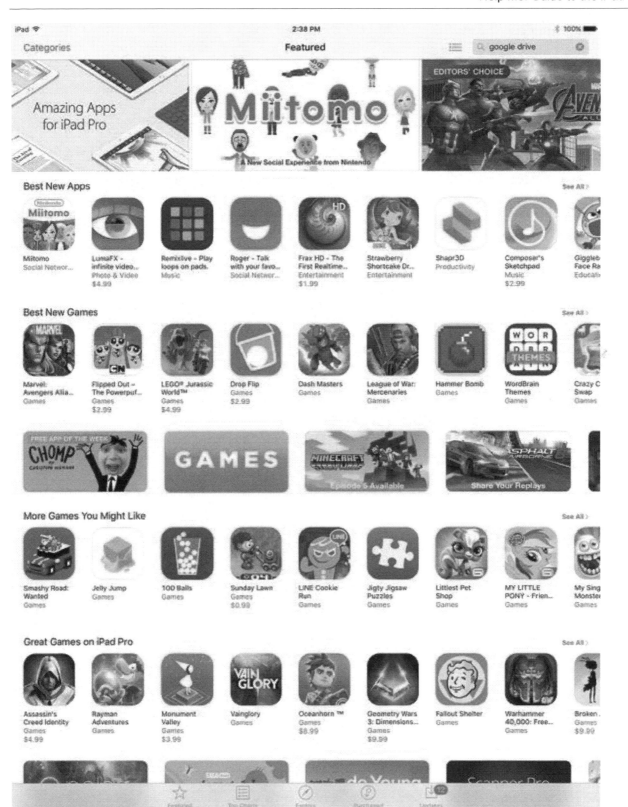

Figure 4: Application Store

Browse by Category

To browse applications by category:

1. Touch the icon. The Application Store opens.
2. Touch **Categories** at the top of the screen. The Categories window appears, as shown in **Figure 5**. Touch the screen and move your finger up or down to scroll through the categories.
3. Touch a category to browse it. Some categories have sub-categories. Repeat step 2 to find the sub-category that you need.

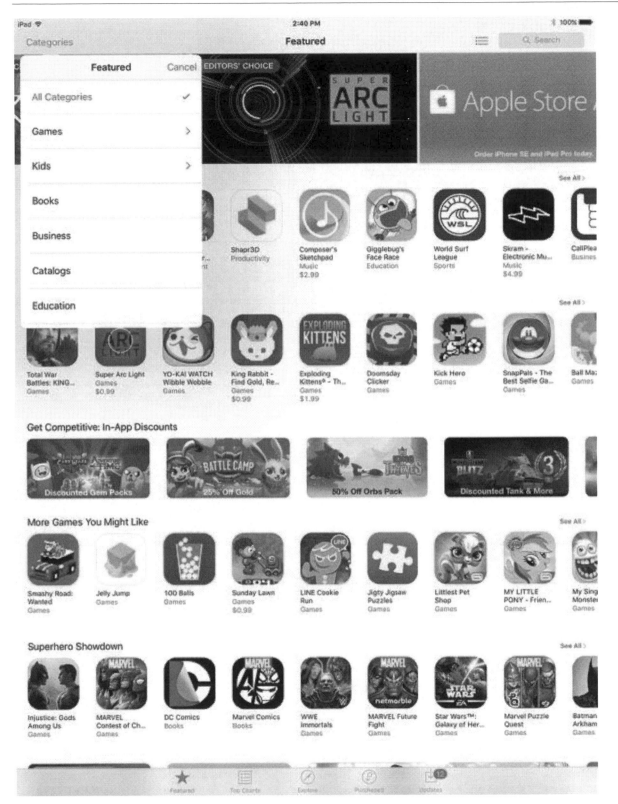

Figure 5: Categories Window

Browse by Popularity

To browse applications by popularity:

1. Touch the ⬛ icon. The Application Store opens.
2. Touch the ⬛ icon at the bottom of the screen. The Top Charts screen appears, as shown in **Figure 6**. The top Paid and Free applications appear by default.
3. Touch **Top Grossing** to view the most popular applications that have earned their creators the most money. Some Top Grossing apps are free, but in-app purchases are considered when calculating the top grossing applications.

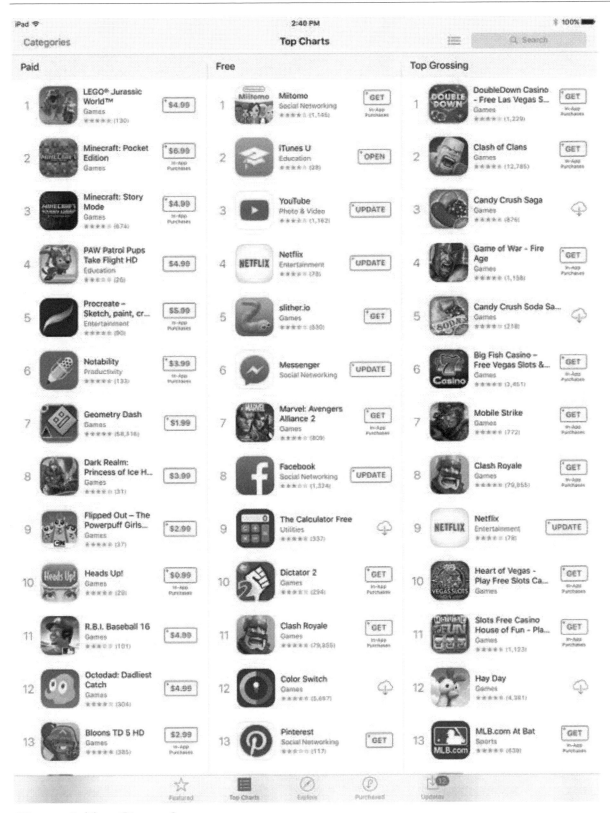

Figure 6: Top Charts Screen

5. Buying an Application

You may purchase applications directly from your iPad. To buy an application:

1. Touch the icon. The Application Store opens.
2. Find an application. Refer to *"Searching for an Application to Purchase"* on page 174 to learn how.
3. Touch an application in the list. The Application description appears, as shown in **Figure 7**.
4. Touch the price of the application, or touch **GET**, next to the name of the application. 'BUY' appears if the application is paid or 'INSTALL' if the application is free. If the application is already downloaded to your iPad, 'INSTALLED' appears.
   Touch **BUY** or **INSTALL**. The password prompt appears.
5. Enter your iTunes password and touch **OK**. The iPad returns to the Home screen, and the application is downloaded and installed.

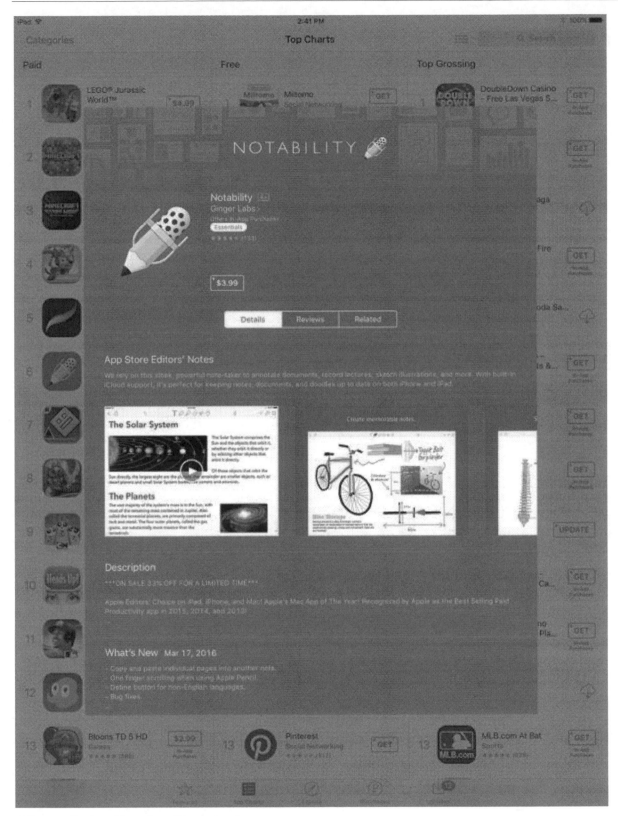

Figure 7: Application Description

6. Using Wi-Fi to Download an Application

Applications that are over 10MB in size require the iPad to connect to a Wi-Fi network to download. These applications will display the following message: "Application over 10MB. Connect to a Wi-Fi network or use iTunes on your computer to download >APP NAME<", where APP NAME refers to the name of the application you are trying to download. Refer to *"Using Wi-Fi"* on page 19 to learn how to turn on Wi-Fi.

7. Switching Between Applications

The iPad allows you to switch between running applications without having to exit any of them. For instance, you can listen to Pandora radio and read an eBook at the same time. To switch between applications:

1. Touch an application icon on one of your Home screens. The application opens.
2. Press the **Home** button. The Home screen is shown.
3. Open another application.
4. Press the **Home** button twice quickly. All of the open applications are displayed, as shown in **Figure 8**.
5. Touch an application icon. The iPad switches to the selected application.

Note: When switching to another application, the first application is never automatically closed. The application is simply running in the background. Refer to "Closing an Application Running in the Background" *on page 184 to learn how to close an application.*

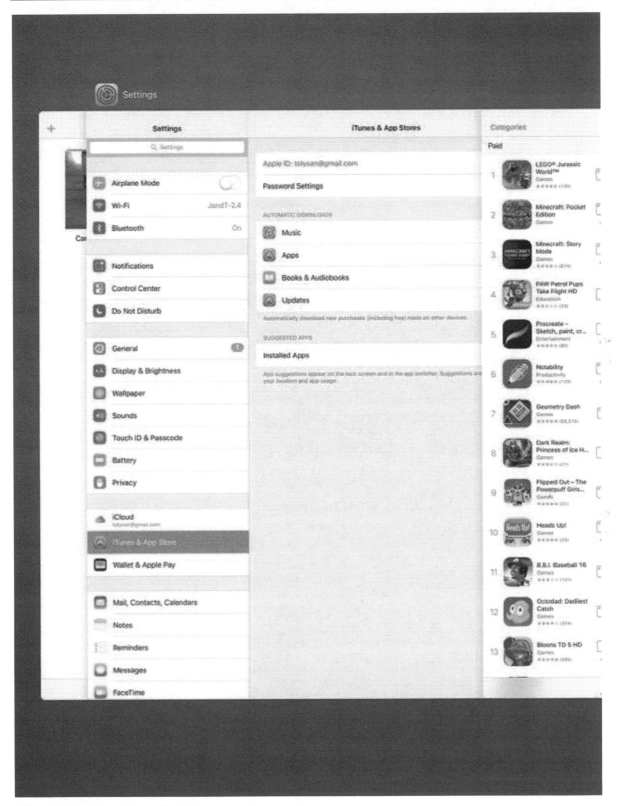

Figure 8: Open Applications

8. Closing an Application Running in the Background

After pressing the Home button to exit an application, it is not closed, but is left running in the background instead. It is good to have the application running, because you can always switch to it quickly. However, if an application stops responding or if your battery is dying too quickly, you may wish to close it. To close an application running in the background, press the **Home** button twice quickly. All of the open applications are displayed. Touch and hold an application icon and slide your finger up. The application is closed. You can also close multiple applications at the same time by touching two or more applications and sliding your fingers up.

9. Organizing Applications into Folders

To learn how to organize applications into folders, refer to *"Creating an Icon Folder"* on page 17.

10. Reading User Reviews

In order to make a more informed decision when purchasing an application, you can read the reviews written by other users. However, be aware that people who have not used the application can also post reviews, which are uninformed. To read user reviews for an application:

1. Touch the ![icon] icon. The Application Store opens.
2. Find an application. Refer to *"Searching for an Application to Purchase"* on page 174 to learn how.
3. Touch an application icon. The Application description appears.
4. Touch **Reviews** below the name of the application. The reviews for the application appear.

11. Changing Application Settings

Some applications have settings that can be changed from the Settings screen. To change the Application settings, touch the ![icon] icon. The Settings screen appears. Touch an application below 'Game Center' at the bottom of the screen. The Application Settings screen appears. The settings on this screen depend on the particular application.

12. Deleting an Application

You may delete most applications from your iPad to free up space on your memory card or Home screen. To delete an unwanted application:

1. Touch and hold an application icon. All of the applications on the Home screen begin to shake. Applications that can be erased have an ⊗ button in their top left corner.

2. Touch the ⊗ button next to an application icon. A confirmation dialog appears.

3. Touch **Delete**. A confirmation dialog may appear regarding Game Center data, which includes achievements and other game data. Touch **Remove** to delete this data, or touch **Keep** to keep it. The application is deleted.

4. Press the **Home** button. The application icons stop shaking and the ⊗ buttons disappear.

Note: If you delete a paid application, you can download it again free of charge at any time. Refer to "Buying an Application" on page 180, and follow the instructions for buying the application to re-download it.

13. Sending an Application as a Gift

On iPads, applications can be sent as gifts. The recipient receives an email notification, and can then download the gifted application from the Application Store. To send an application as a gift:

1. Touch the ⊞ icon. The Application Store opens.

2. Find the application that you want to give as a gift. Refer to *"Searching for an Application to Purchase"* on page 174 to learn how.

3. Touch the application icon. The application description appears.

4. Touch the ⬆ icon in the upper right-hand corner of the screen. The Application options appear, as shown in **Figure 9**.

5. Touch **Gift**. The Send Gift screen appears, as shown in **Figure 10**.

6. Touch **To:** and enter the email address of the recipient of the gift. Enter an optional message.

7. Touch **Today** to select when the gift should be shared, if the date is other than the current day.

8. Touch **Next**. The Theme Selection screen appears.

9. Select a theme and touch **Next** at the top of the screen. The Gift Confirmation screen appears, as shown in **Figure 11**.

10. Touch **Buy** at the top of the screen. 'BUY NOW' appears as a confirmation.

11. Touch **BUY NOW**. The password prompt appears.

12. Enter your iTunes password and touch **OK**. The gift is purchased and sent.

Note: You are charged for the gifted application as soon as you purchase it.

Figure 9: Application Options

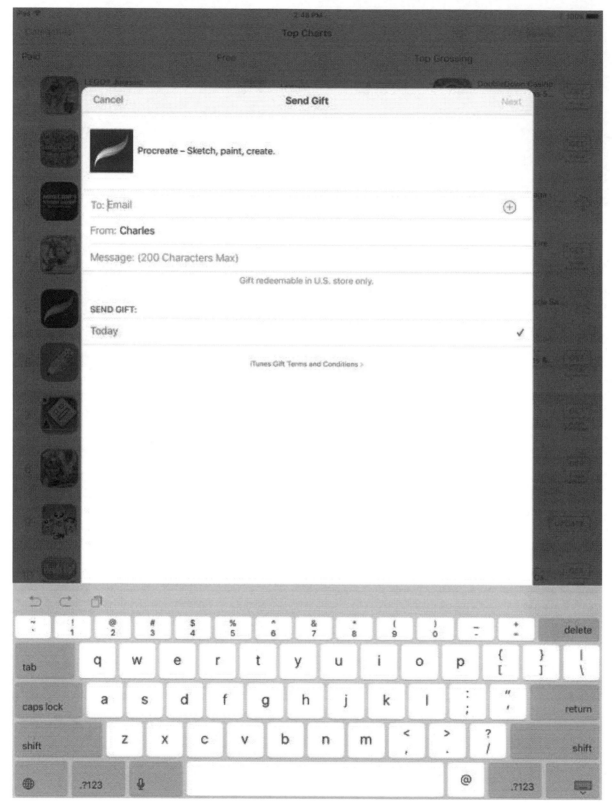

Figure 10: Send Gift Screen

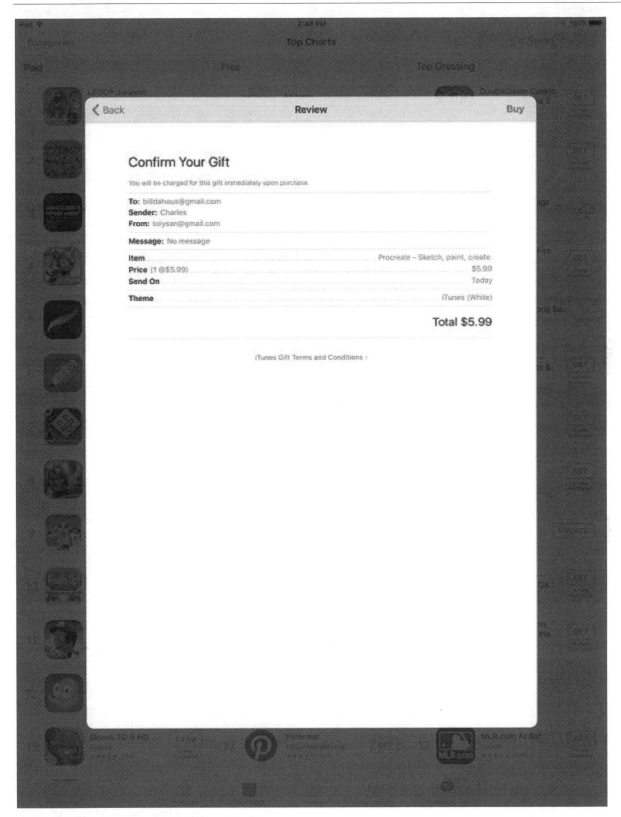

Figure 11: Gift Confirmation Screen

14. Redeeming a Gifted Application

When receiving an application as a gift, you must redeem it in order to download it. To redeem a gift and download the application using your iPad:

1. Touch the icon. The email application opens.
2. Touch the email with the subject '**NAME sent you an iTunes Gift**', where NAME represents the name of the sender. The email opens. Refer to *"Reading Email"* on page 146 to learn how to find an email.
3. Touch the **Redeem Now** button in the email. The Application Store opens.
4. Touch **Redeem** at the top of the screen. The gifted application is downloaded and installed. If the application is over 10MB, you must first turn on Wi-Fi. Refer to *"Using Wi-Fi"* on page 19 to learn how to turn Wi-Fi on. If this is your first time downloading an application from the iTunes store, you will need to touch **Agree** several times to accept several pages of terms and conditions.

15. Turning Automatic Application Updates On or Off

The iPad can automatically download updates for applications when new versions are released. To turn automatic application updates on or off:

1. Touch the icon. The Settings screen appears.
2. Touch **iTunes & App Store**. The iTunes & App Store Settings screen appears.

3. Touch the switch next to 'Updates' under 'Automatic Downloads'. The switch appears Automatic application updates are turned on.
4. Touch the switch next to 'Updates' under 'Automatic Downloads'. The switch appears Automatic application updates are turned off.

16. Using Slide Over to Multitask

You can reference an application while using another by opening a second application on the right side of the screen. Only certain applications are compatible with this feature, which is called Slide Over.

To use slide over, turn on the feature first. To turn on slide over:

1. Touch the ⊚ icon. The Settings screen appears.
2. Touch **General**. The General Settings screen appears, as shown in **Figure 12**.
3. Touch **Multitasking**. The Multitasking Settings screen appears, as shown in **Figure 13**.
4. Touch the ⬭ switch next to 'Allow Multiple Apps'. The ⬤ switch appears and Slide Over is turned on. Turn the feature off by touching the ⬤ switch.

To use slide over:

1. Touch the right-hand side of the screen at any time, and slide your finger to the left. The Slide Over Application window appears, as shown in **Figure 14**.
2. Touch an application in the list. The application opens in the window on the right-hand side of the screen.
3. To select another application, touch the black stripe at the top of the window, and slide your finger down. A list of applications appears.
4. To hide the Slide Over window, touch the screen anywhere outside of the window.

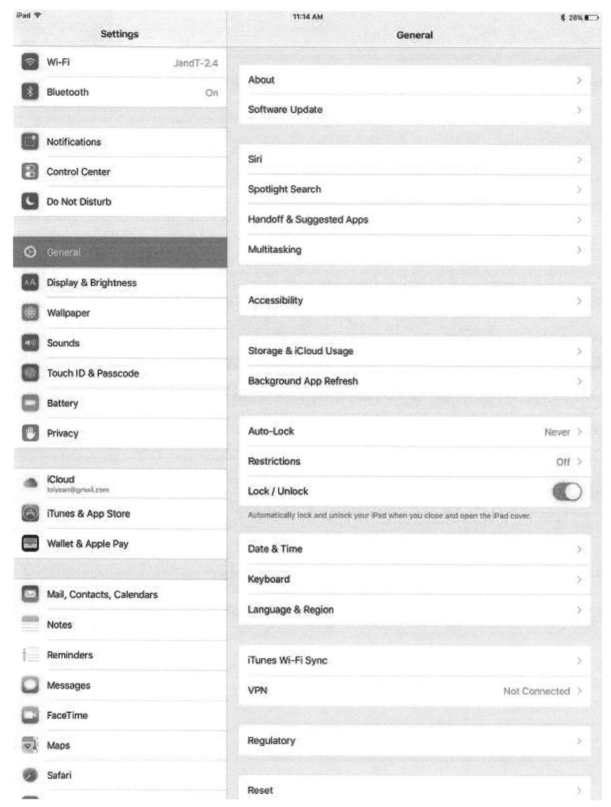

Figure 12: General Settings Screen

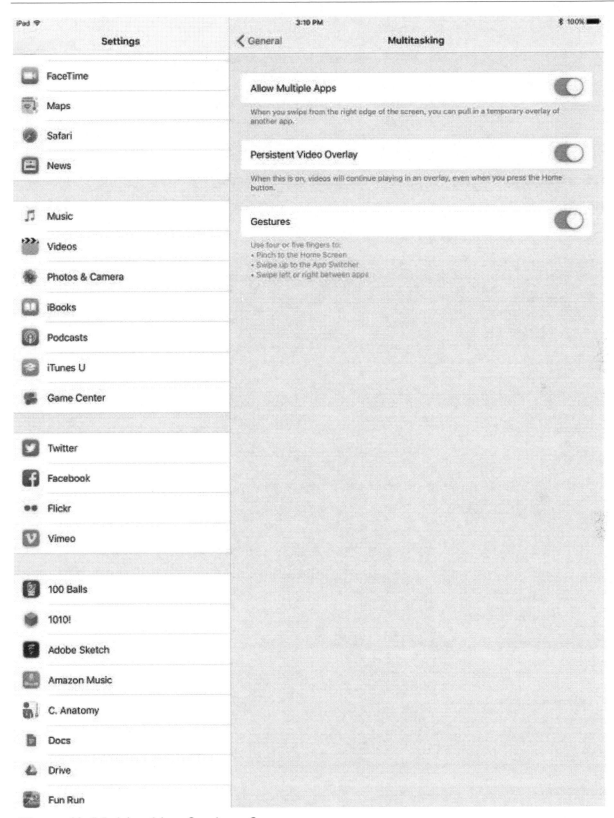

Figure 13: Multitasking Settings Screen

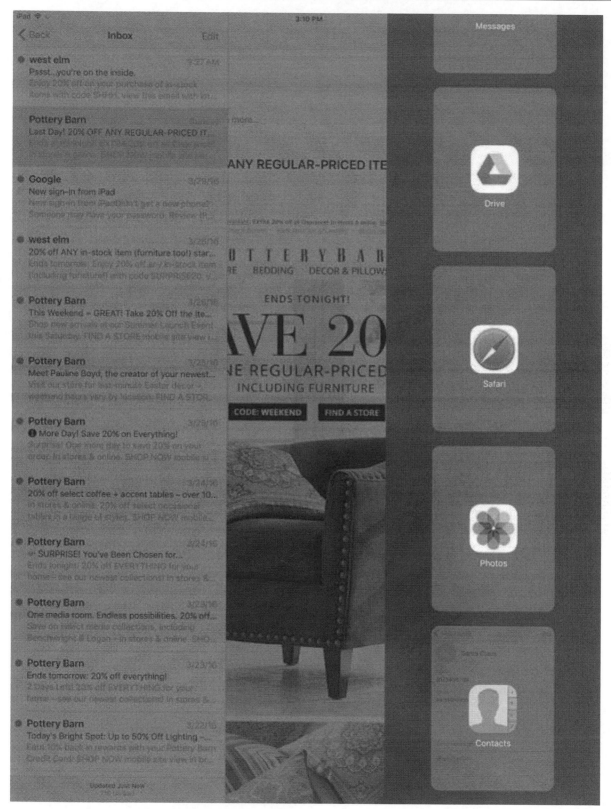

Figure 14: Slide Over Application Window

17. Using Side-by-Side to Multitask

The iPad Pro lets you use two applications on one screen, stacked side-by-side. As with Slide Over, only certain applications are compatible with this feature. To use Side-by-Side to multitask, turn on this feature. To turn on Side-by-Side:

1. Touch the ⚙ icon. The Settings screen appears.
2. Touch **General**. The General Settings screen appears.
3. Touch **Multitasking**. The Multitasking Settings screen appears.
4. Touch the ⬭ switch next to 'Allow Multiple Apps'. The ⬤ switch appears and Slide Over is turned on. Turn the feature off by touching the ⬤ switch.

To use side-by-side:

1. Touch the right-hand side of the screen at any time, and slide your finger to the left. The Slide Over Application window appears.
2. Touch an application in the list. The application opens in the window on the right-hand side of the screen.
3. Touch the white divider between the two applications, and slide your finger to the left. The two applications appear side-by-side.
4. To open one of the applications in full screen, touch the white divider, and slide your finger to the left or right.

Using Siri

Siri is a voice assistant that comes with every iPad. Follow the tips in this chapter to use Siri to its full potential.

Table of Contents

Note: These phrases are only suggestions. Siri is flexible, and you can use many synonymous phrases.

1. Making a FaceTime Call Using Siri

To make a call using Siri, press and hold the **Home** button and wait for Siri to speak. Say one of the following phrases:

- FaceTime Call John (use any name)

- Call 123 555 1345

- FaceTime Call home

- FaceTime Jacob

2. Sending and Receiving Text Messages Using Siri

To send, read, or reply to a text message using Siri, press and hold the **Home** button and wait for Siri to speak. Say one of the following phrases:

- Tell Anne See you soon
- Send a message to Rob Burr
- Send a message to Larry saying What's your address?
- Send a message to Julie on her mobile saying I got an iPad 6!
- Send a message to 999 555 2222
- Text Jude and Prudence What are you guys up to today?
- Read my new messages
- Read it again
- Reply that's great news
- Tell him ETA is 20 minutes
- Call her

3. Managing the Address Book Using Siri

To manage the address book using Siri, press and hold the **Home** button and wait for Siri to speak. Say one of the following phrases:

- What's Joe's address?
- What is Susan Park's phone number?
- When is my grandfather's birthday?
- Show Bobby's email address
- Show Pete Abred
- Find people named Apple
- My brother is Trudy Ages (assigns a relationship to the name)
- Who is Colin Card? (indicates Colin Card's relationship to you)
- Call my brother at home (calls the number assigned to the relationship)

4. Setting Up and Managing Meetings Using Siri

To set up and manage meetings using Siri, press and hold the **Home** button and wait for Siri to speak. Say one of the following phrases:

- Set up a meeting at 10
- Set up a meeting with Zoe at 9
- Meet with Nikki at noon
- New appointment with Dan Delion Tuesday at 4
- Schedule a focus group meeting at 3:30 today in the boardroom
- Move my 2pm meeting to 3:30
- Add Wendy to my meeting with Waldo
- Cancel the focus group meeting
- What does the rest of my day look like?
- What's on my calendar for Monday?
- When is my next appointment?
- Where is my next meeting?

5. Checking the Time and Setting Alarms Using Siri

To check the time and set alarms using Siri, press and hold the **Home** button and wait for Siri to speak. Say one of the following phrases:

- Wake me up tomorrow at 6am
- Set an alarm for 6:30am
- Wake me up in 8 hours
- Change my 5:30 alarm to 6:30
- Turn off my 4:30 alarm
- What time is it?
- What time is it in Moscow?
- What is today's date?
- What's the date this Friday?
- Set the timer for 30 minutes
- Show the timer
- Pause the timer
- Resume
- Reset the timer
- Stop it

6. Sending and Receiving Email Using Siri

To send and receive email using Siri, press and hold the **Home** button and wait for Siri to speak. Say one of the following phrases:

- Email Dave about the trip
- Email New email to John Diss
- Mail Dad about dinner
- Email Dr. Spaulding and say Got your message
- Mail Jack and Jill about the party and say It was awesome
- Check email
- Any new email from Mom today?
- Show new mail about the apartment
- Show the email from Roger yesterday
- Reply Dear Mark I'm sorry for your loss

7. Getting Directions and Finding Businesses Using Siri

To get directions and find businesses using Siri, press and hold the **Home** button and wait for Siri to speak. Say one of the following phrases:

- How do I get home?
- Show 10 Park Ave. Boston Massachusetts
- Directions to my parents' home
- Find coffee near me
- Where is the closest Starbucks?
- Find a Mexican restaurant in New Mexico
- Find a gas station within walking distance

8. Playing Music Using Siri

To play music using Siri, press and hold the **Home** button and wait for Siri to speak. Say one of the following phrases:

- Play Hotel California
- Play Coldplay shuffled
- Play Dave Matthews Band
- Play some folk
- Play my roadtrip playlist
- Shuffle my party playlist
- Play
- Pause
- Skip

9. Searching the Web and Asking Questions

To search the web using Siri, press and hold the **Home** button and wait for Siri to speak. Say one of the following phrases:

- Search the web for Apple News
- Search for chili recipes
- Google the humane society
- Search Wikipedia for Duckbilled Platypus
- Bing Secondhand Serenade
- How many calories in a doughnut?
- What is an 18% tip on $180.45 for six people?
- How long do cats live?
- What's 25 squared?
- How many dollars is 60 euros?
- How many days until Christmas?
- When is the next solar eclipse?
- Show me the Ursula Major constellation
- What is the meaning of life?
- What's the price of gasoline in Boston?

10. Looking Up Words in the Dictionary

To look up words using Siri, press and hold the **Home** button and wait for Siri to speak. Say one of the following phrases:

- What is the meaning of meticulous?
- Define albeit
- Look up the word jargon

Adjusting Wireless Settings

Table of Contents

1. Turning Airplane Mode On or Off

Most airplanes do not allow wireless communications while in flight. Continue using the iPad by enabling Airplane mode before take-off. You may not place or receive calls, send or receive text messages or emails, or surf the Web while in Airplane mode. Airplane Mode is also useful when traveling outside of your area of service to avoid any roaming charges and to preserve battery life. To turn Airplane Mode on or off:

1. Touch the icon. The Settings screen appears, as shown in **Figure 1**.

2. Touch the ⬯ switch next to 'Airplane Mode'. The ⬯ switch appears and Airplane mode is turned on.

3. Touch the ⬯ switch next to 'Airplane Mode'. The ⬯ switch appears and Airplane mode is turned off.

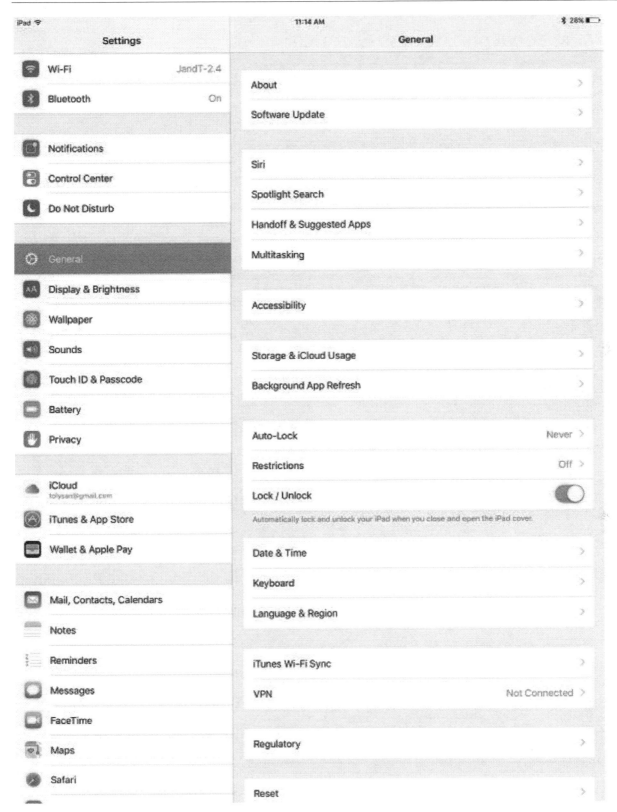

Figure 1: Settings Screen

2. Turning Location Services On or Off

Some applications, such as Maps, require the Location Services feature to be turned on, which determines your current location. To turn Location Services on or off:

1. Touch the icon. The Settings screen appears.
2. Scroll down and touch **Privacy**. The Privacy Settings screen appears, as shown in **Figure 2**.
3. Touch **Location Services**. The Location Services screen appears, as shown in **Figure 3**.

4. Touch the switch next to 'Location Services'. The switch appears and Location Services are turned on.

5. Touch the switch next to 'Location Services'. The switch appears and Location Services are turned off.

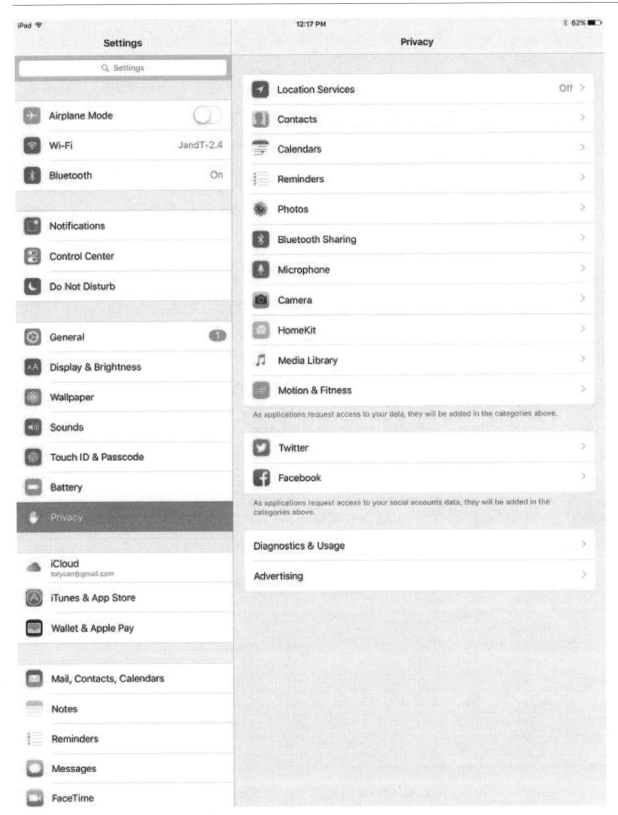

Figure 2: Privacy Settings Screen

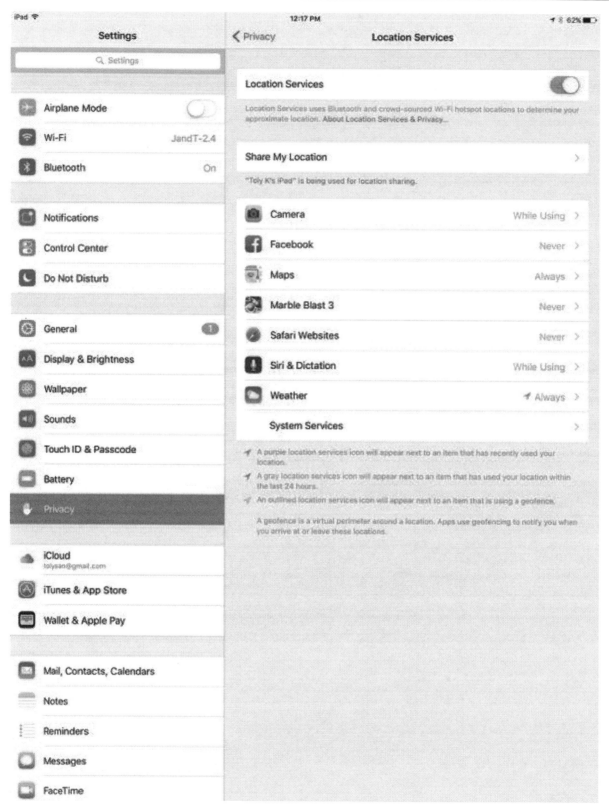

Figure 3: Location Services Screen

3. Customizing Cellular Data Usage (iPad 4G only)

To surf the internet and download applications when not connected to Wi-Fi, you need to turn on cellular data. However, you can turn off cellular data if you wish to conserve battery life in an area with little or no 4G service. To turn cellular data on or off:

1. Touch the ⊚ icon. The Settings screen appears.
2. Touch **Cellular**. The Cellular Settings screen appears.
3. Touch the ⬭ switch next to 'Cellular Data'. The ⬤ switch appears and cellular data is turned on.
4. Touch the ⬤ switch next to 'Cellular Data'. The ⬭ switch appears and cellular data is turned off.

You may also manage the cellular data usage from the Cellular Settings screen. To manage cellular data usage:

1. Touch the ⬤ switch next to 'Mail', 'Passbook', or another application. Cellular data is turned off for the corresponding application.
2. Touch the ⬭ switch next to the name of an application. Cellular data is turned on for the corresponding application.
3. Touch **System Services** to view the amount of data used by each service on your iPad.

4. Turning Data Roaming On or Off (iPad 4G only)

When you are in an area with no 4G coverage, the iPad can use the Data Roaming feature to acquire signal from other networks. Be aware that Data Roaming can be extremely costly. Contact your network provider for details. To turn Data Roaming on or off:

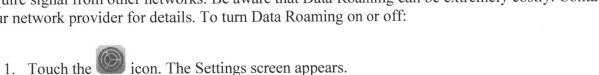

1. Touch the ⊚ icon. The Settings screen appears.
2. Touch **Cellular**. The Cellular Settings screen appears.
3. Touch the ⬭ switch next to 'Data Roaming'. The ⬤ switch appears and Data Roaming is turned on.

4. Touch the switch next to 'Data Roaming'. The switch appears and Data Roaming is turned off.

5. Setting Up a Virtual Private Network (VPN)

You can use your iPad to connect to an external network, such as a corporate one. To set up a VPN:

1. Touch the icon. The Settings screen appears.
2. Touch **General**. The General Settings screen appears, as shown in **Figure 4**.
3. Scroll down and touch **VPN**. The VPN screen appears, as shown in **Figure 5**.
4. Touch **Add VPN Configuration**. The Add Configuration screen appears, as shown in **Figure 6**.
5. Touch each field and enter the required information. Touch **Save** at the top of the screen when you are finished. The VPN is set up.

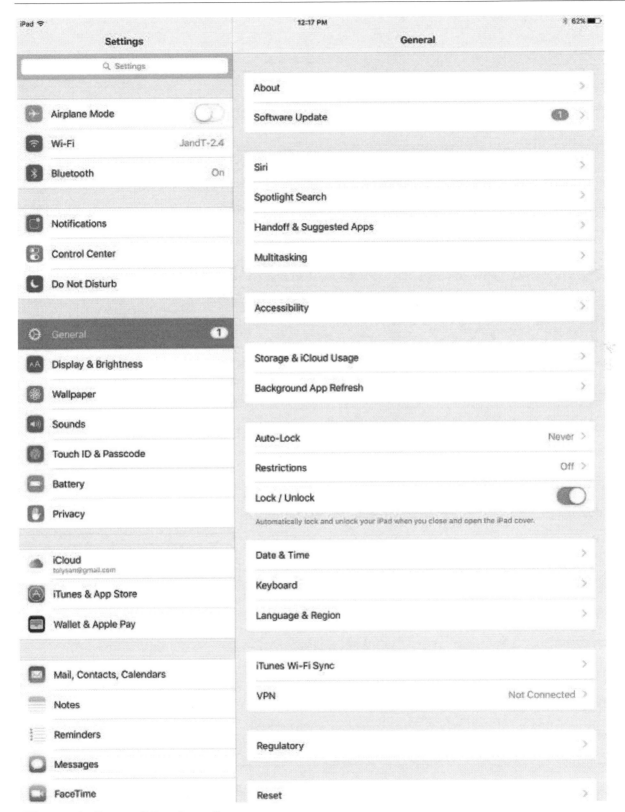

Figure 4: General Settings Screen

Figure 5: VPN Screen

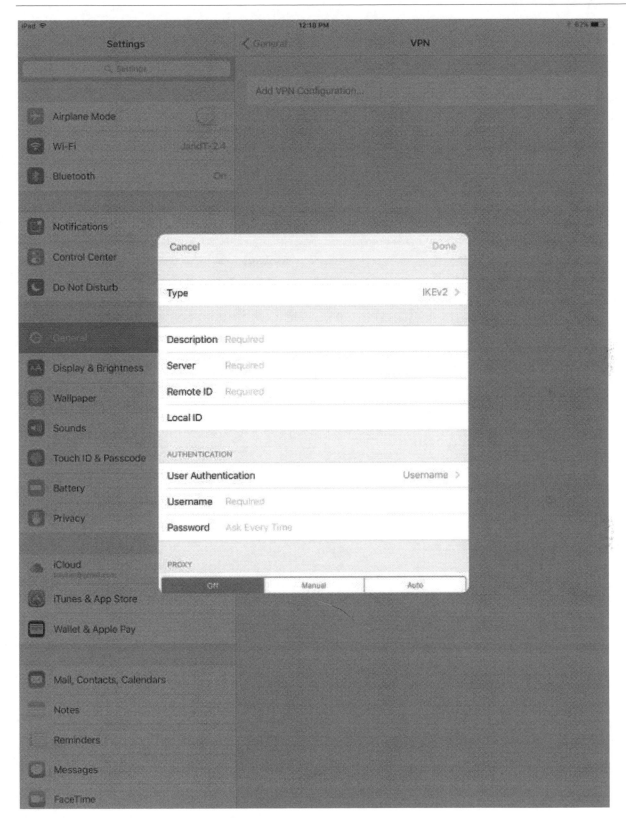

Figure 6: Add Configuration Screen

6. Turning Bluetooth On or Off

A wireless Bluetooth headset or keyboard can be used with the iPad. Be aware that leaving Bluetooth turned on while the headset or keyboard is not in use decreases battery life. To turn Bluetooth on or off:

1. Touch the ![icon] icon. The Settings screen appears.
2. Touch **Bluetooth**. The Bluetooth Settings screen appears, as shown in **Figure 7**.
3. Touch the ![switch] switch next to 'Bluetooth'. Bluetooth is turned on and a list of available devices appears. If there are no Bluetooth devices near the iPad, the list will be empty. Make sure that each Bluetooth device to which you want to connect is discoverable. Refer to the device's manual to find out how to turn on Bluetooth and make it discoverable.
4. Touch the ![switch] switch next to 'Bluetooth'. Bluetooth is turned off.

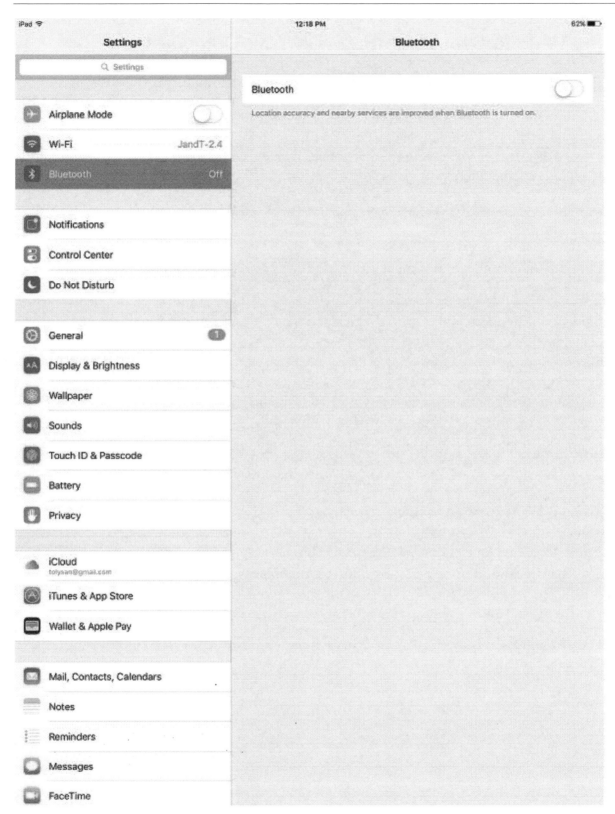

Figure 7: Bluetooth Settings Screen

7. Using Wi-Fi to Sync Your iPad with Your Computer

Syncing your iPad with your computer allows you save your media library on your computer in case you have to erase your iPad, or if you buy a new iPad. Instead of connecting your iPad to your computer to sync music, applications, and other media, you may sync wirelessly using Wi-Fi. Before you can use this feature, you must turn it on using iTunes on your computer. Refer to **https://www.apple.com/support/itunes/** if you need help using iTunes. To use Wi-Fi to sync your iPad with your computer:

Note: You may only use Wi-Fi syncing when your iPad is plugged in to an outlet, and Wi-Fi is turned on.

1. Connect your iPad to your computer using the cable that was provided when you purchased it. On some computers, iTunes opens automatically. If it does not, open iTunes.
2. Click the name of the iPad, or   icon at the top or left side of the screen, depending on the version of iTunes. The iPad information screen appears, as shown in **Figure 8**. You may need to first click **Continue**, and then click **Get Started** before this screen appears.
3. Click **Sync with this iPadNAME over Wi-Fi**, where iPadNAME represents the name of your iPad. A check mark appears next to 'Sync with this iPadNAME'.
4. Click **Apply**. The Wi-Fi Sync feature is turned on.
5. Disconnect your iPad from your computer, and plug it into an outlet, as if you are charging it. Your iPad should automatically Sync with your computer. If it does not sync, follow steps 6-9 below.
6. Touch the   icon. The Settings screen appears.
7. Touch **General**. The General Settings screen appears.
8. Scroll down and touch **iTunes Wi-Fi Sync**. The iTunes Wi-Fi Sync screen appears.
9. Touch **Sync Now**. Your iPad syncs with your computer.

iPad Pro

Capacity: 26.38 GB
Serial Number: DLXR4LSFGMLG

iOS 9.3

A newer version of the iPad software is available (version 9.3.1). To update your iPad with the latest software, click Update.

[Update] [Restore iPad...]

Backups

Automatically Back Up

◉ **iCloud**
  Back up the most important data on your iPad to iCloud.

○ **This computer**
  A full backup of your iPad will be stored on this computer.

  ☐ **Encrypt local backup**
  This will allow account passwords, Health, and HomeKit data to be backed up.

  [Change Password...]

Manually Back Up and Restore

Manually back up your iPad to this computer or restore a backup stored on this computer.

[Back Up Now] [Restore Backup...]

Latest Backup:
4/6/2016 9:27 AM to iCloud

Options

☐ **Open iTunes when this iPad is connected**

☐ **Sync with this iPad over Wi-Fi**

☐ **Sync only checked songs and videos**

☐ **Prefer standard definition videos**

☐ **Convert higher bit rate songs to** [128 kbps ◇] **AAC**

☐ **Manually manage music and videos**

[Reset Warnings]

[Configure Accessibility...]

Figure 8: iPad Information Screen

Adjusting Sound Settings

Table of Contents

1. Turning Volume Button Functionality On or Off

The volume buttons can be used to adjust the volume of the media, alerts, and the ringer. When the volume button functionality is disabled, they no longer work. To turn the volume button functionality on or off:

1. Touch the ⚙ icon. The Settings screen appears, as shown in **Figure 1**.
2. Scroll down and touch **Sounds**. The Sound Settings screen appears, as shown in **Figure 2**.
3. Touch the 🔘 switch next to 'Change with Buttons' under the 'Ringer and Alerts' section. The ⚪ switch appears and volume button functionality is turned off.
4. Touch the ⚪ switch next to 'Change with Buttons'. The 🔘 switch appears and the volume button functionality is turned on.

Figure 1: Settings Screen

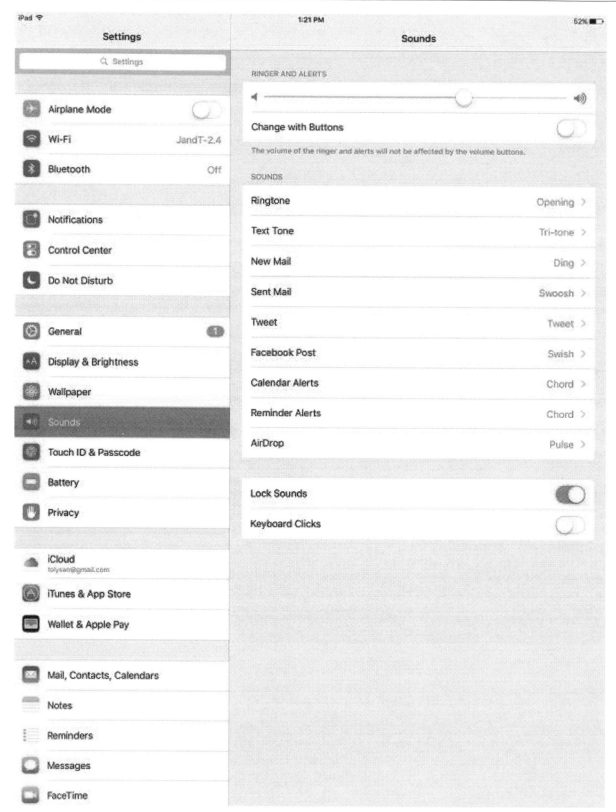

Figure 2: Sound Settings Screen

2. Setting the Default Ringtone

You may change the ringtone that sounds every time somebody calls you (FaceTime only on an iPad). To set a default ringtone:

1. Touch the ⊚ icon. The Settings screen appears.
2. Touch **Sounds**. The Sound Settings screen appears.
3. Touch **Ringtone**. A list of ringtones appears, as shown in **Figure 3**.
4. Touch a ringtone. The new default ringtone is selected and a preview plays.
5. Touch **Sounds** at the top of the screen. The new ringtone is set as the default.

*Note: You can also touch **Store** at the top of the screen to purchase more ringtones.*

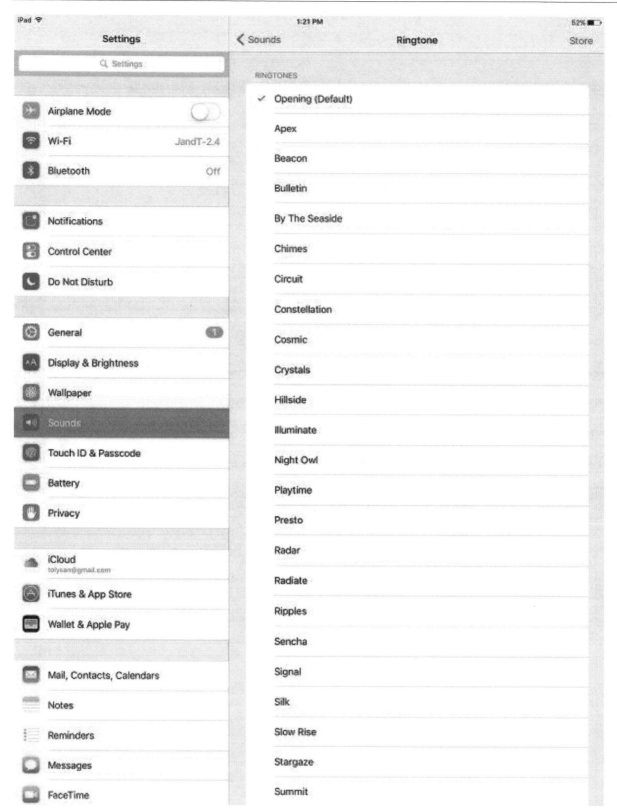

Figure 3: List of Ringtones

3. Customizing Notification and Alert Sounds

There are several notification and alert sounds that can be changed on the iPad. To customize notification and alert sounds:

1. Touch the ⊚ icon. The Settings screen appears.
2. Touch **Sounds**. The Sound Settings screen appears.
3. Touch one of the following options to change the corresponding sound:

   - **Text Tone** - Plays when a new text message arrives.

   - **New Mail** - Plays when a new email arrives.

   - **Sent Mail** - Plays when an email is sent from the iPad.

   - **Tweet** - Plays when a new Tweet arrives.

   - **Facebook Post** - Plays when one of your Facebook friends creates a new post.

   - **Calendar Alerts** - Plays as a reminder for a calendar event.

   - **Reminder Alerts** - Plays as a notification of a previously set reminder.

4. Turning Lock Sounds On or Off

The iPad can make a sound every time that it is locked or unlocked. By default, this sound is turned on. To turn Lock Sounds on or off:

1. Touch the ⊚ icon. The Settings screen appears.
2. Touch **Sounds**. The Sound Settings screen appears.
3. Scroll down and touch the ⬤ switch next to 'Lock Sounds'. The ◯ switch appears and lock sounds are turned off.
4. Touch the ◯ switch next to 'Lock Sounds'. The ⬤ switch appears and lock sounds are turned on.

5. Turning Keyboard Clicks On or Off

The iPad can make a sound every time a key is touched on the virtual keyboard. By default, keyboard clicks are turned on. To turn Keyboard Clicks on or off:

1. Touch the icon. The Settings screen appears.
2. Touch **Sounds**. The Sound Settings screen appears.

3. Touch the switch next to 'Keyboard Clicks'. The switch appears and Keyboard Clicks are turned off.

4. Touch the switch next to 'Keyboard Clicks'. The switch appears and Keyboard Clicks are turned on.

Adjusting Language and Keyboard Settings

Table of Contents

1. Customizing Spelling and Grammar Settings

Customize the Spelling and Grammar settings on your iPad to improve typing accuracy when composing text messages or emails. To customize the Spelling and Grammar settings:

1. Touch the ⚙ icon. The Settings screen appears, as shown in **Figure 1**.
2. Touch **General**. The General Settings screen appears, as shown in **Figure 2**.
3. Scroll down and touch **Keyboard**. The Keyboard Settings screen appears, as shown in **Figure 3**.
4. Touch one of the switches on the right side of the screen to turn the corresponding setting on or off:
   - **Auto-Capitalization** - Capitalizes the first word of every sentence automatically.
   - **Auto-Correction** - Suggests and makes spelling corrections while you type.
   - **Check Spelling** - Underlines all misspelled words.
   - **Enable Caps Lock** - Allows you to turn Caps Lock on by quickly touching the ⬆ key twice on the virtual keyboard. While Caps Lock is turned on, all capital letters are typed without the need to use the ⬆ key.
   - **Predictive** - The Predictive Text feature offers suggestions for the next word in a sentence as you type, which is intelligently based on the words that you have already typed.
   - **"." Shortcut** - Allows a period and an extra space to be inserted when you quickly touch the space bar twice.

Figure 1: Settings Screen

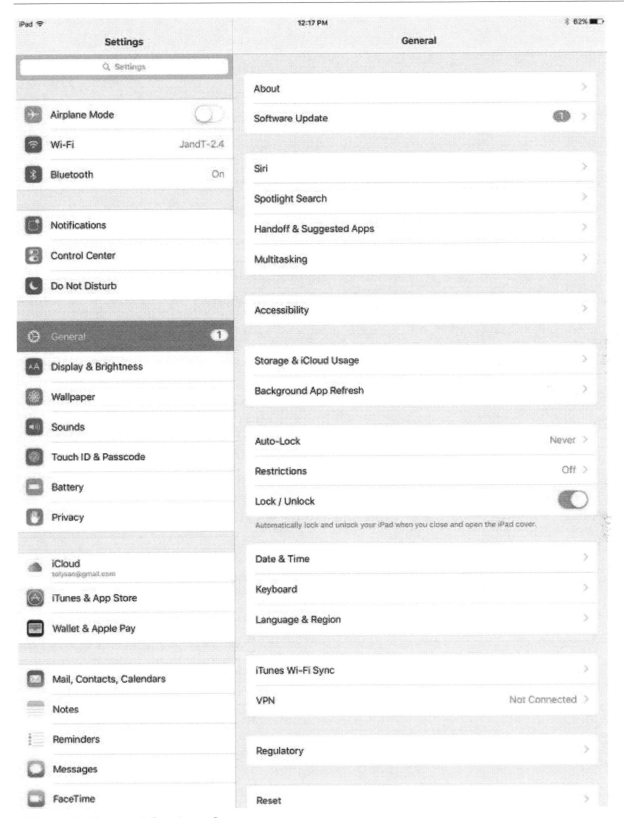

Figure 2: General Settings Screen

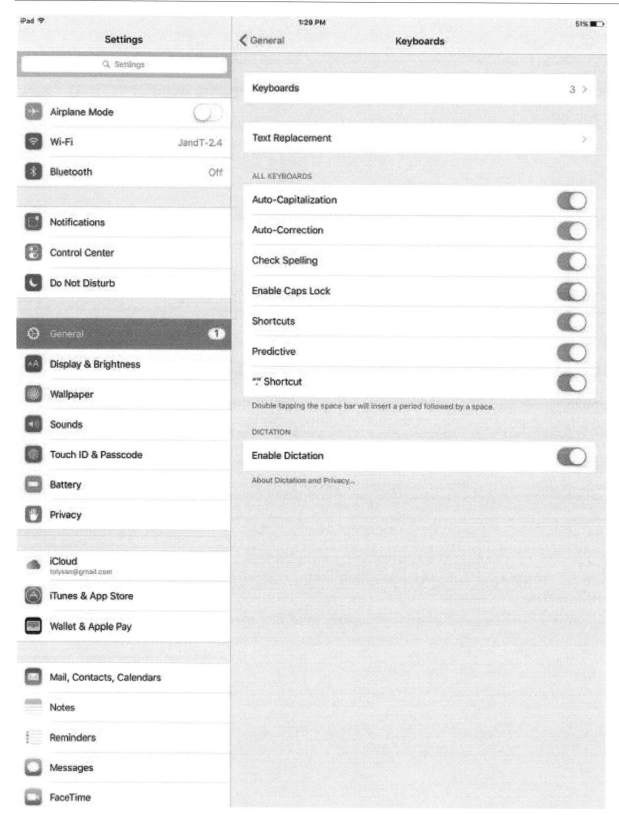

Figure 3: Keyboard Settings Screen

2. Adding an International Keyboard

The iPad allows you to use international keyboards when entering text on the virtual keyboard. To add an international keyboard:

1. Touch the [ ] icon. The Settings screen appears.
2. Touch **General**. The General Settings screen appears.
3. Scroll down and touch **Keyboard**. The Keyboard Settings screen appears.
4. Touch **Keyboards**. The Keyboards screen appears, as shown in **Figure 4**.
5. Touch **Add New Keyboard**. A list of international keyboards appears, as shown in **Figure 5**.
6. Touch a keyboard. The keyboard is added. While typing, touch the [ ] key at the bottom of the virtual keyboard to switch to an international one.
7. You may remove a keyboard from the list by touching and holding it, and then sliding your finger to the left until 'Delete' appears. Touch **Delete** to remove the keyboard.

Note: If you only add the Emoji keyboard (emoticons) in addition to the English keyboard, the

key appears instead of the [ ] *key.*

Figure 4: Keyboards Screen

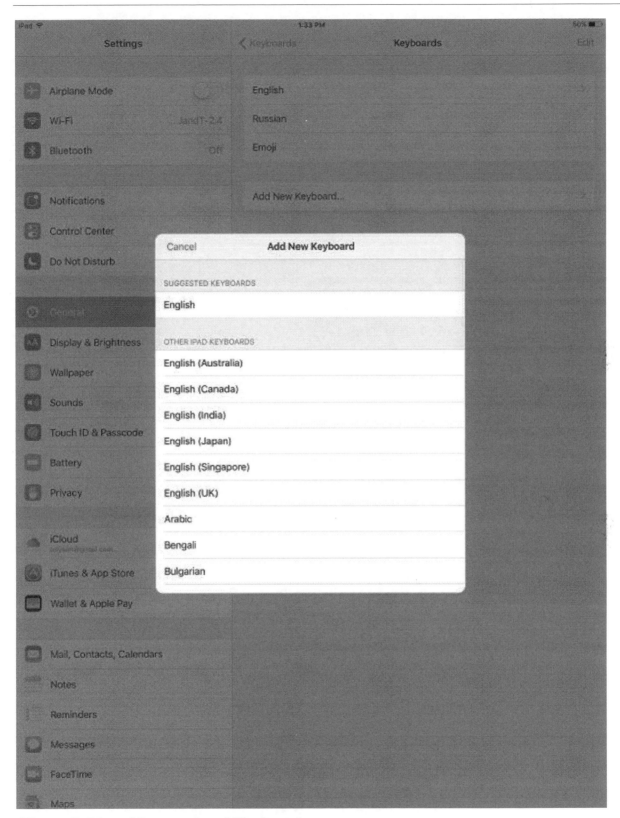

Figure 5: List of International Keyboards

3. Adding a Keyboard Shortcut

The iPad allows you to add custom Keyboard shortcuts. For example, "ur" for "your" or "ttyl" for "talk to you later" are substituted when the corresponding abbreviation is typed. To add a Keyboard shortcut:

1. Touch the [icon] icon. The Settings screen appears.
2. Touch **General**. The General Settings screen appears.
3. Scroll down and touch **Keyboard**. The Keyboard Settings screen appears.
4. Touch **Text Replacement**. A list of existing shortcuts appears, as shown in **Figure 6**.
5. Touch the [+] icon at the top of the screen. The Text Replacement screen appears, as shown in **Figure 7**.
6. Enter the desired phrase to be substituted for the shortcut. Touch **return**.
7. Enter the desired shortcut and touch **Save** at the top of the screen. The keyboard shortcut is added. To use the shortcut, type it and touch the space bar.

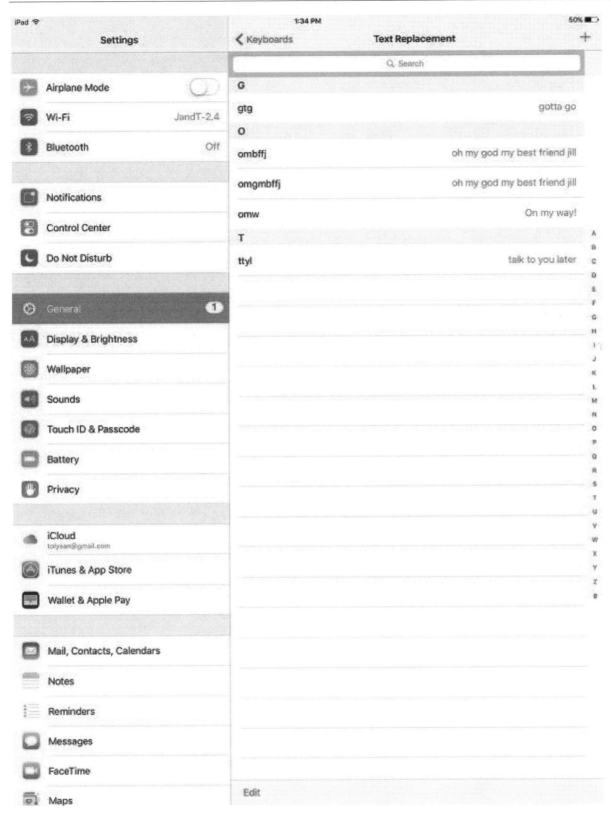

Figure 6: List of Existing Shortcuts

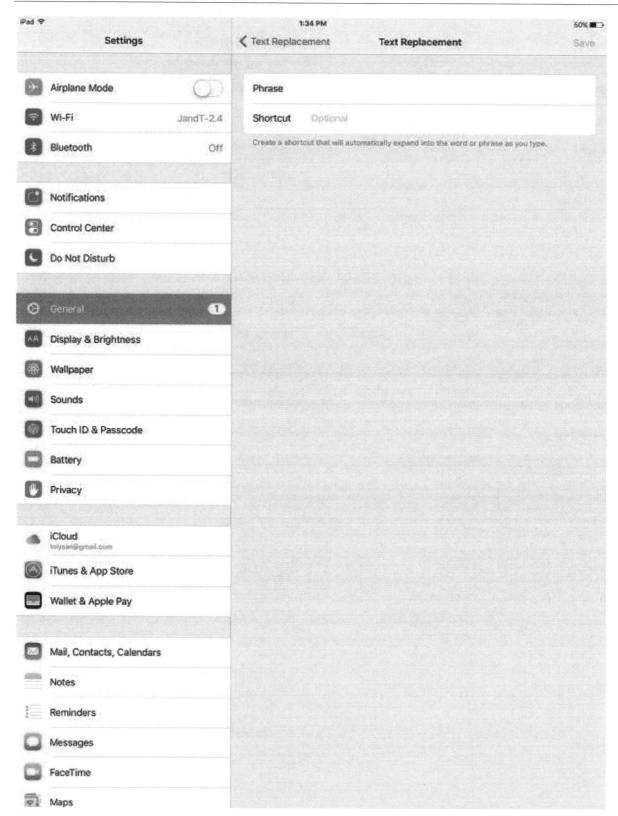

Figure 7: Text Replacement Screen

4. Changing the Operating System Language

The iPad can be changed to display all menus and options in a language other than English. To change the Operating System Language:

1. Touch the ⚙ icon. The Settings screen appears.
2. Touch **General**. The General Settings screen appears.
3. Touch **Language & Region**. The Language & Region screen appears, as shown in **Figure 8**.
4. Touch **iPad Language**, depending on the type of your iPad. A list of available languages appears, as shown in **Figure 9**.
5. Touch a language, and then touch **Done** at the top of the screen. A confirmation dialog appears at the bottom of the screen.
6. Touch **Change to LANGUAGE**, where LANGUAGE is the language that you selected in step 5. The selected language is applied, and all menus and options reflect the change.

Note: It may take some time to install the language. This delay is normal.

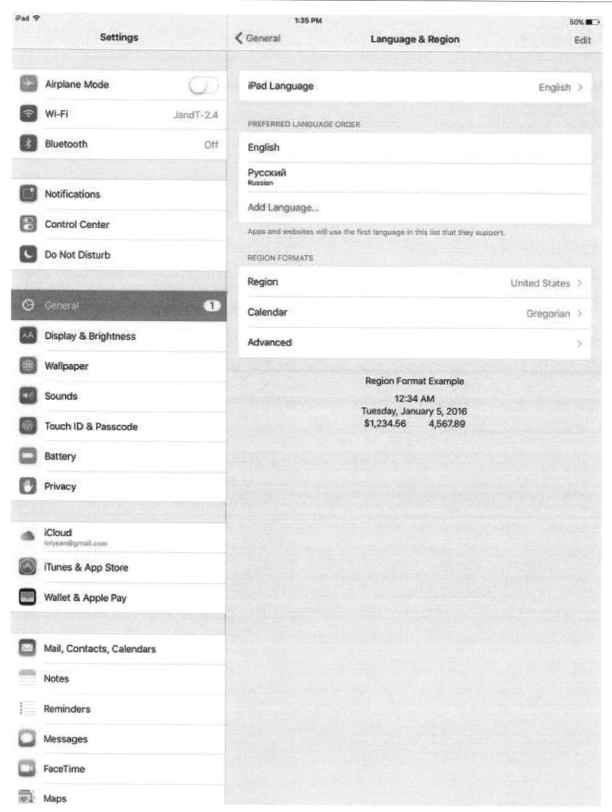

Figure 8: Language & Region Screen

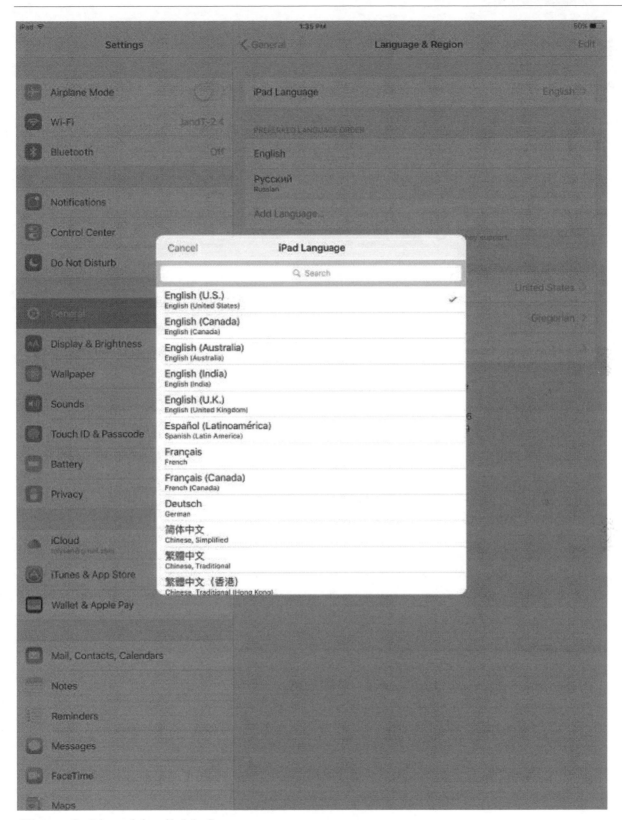

Figure 9: List of Available Languages

5. Changing the Siri Language

You can change the input language that Siri recognizes, as well as the language that she uses to speak. To change the Siri language:

1. Touch the icon. The Settings screen appears.
2. Touch **General**. The General Settings screen appears.
3. Touch **Siri**. The Siri Settings screen appears, as shown in **Figure 10**.
4. Touch **Language**. A list of languages appears.
5. Touch a language. The selected language will be used for Siri.

Note: Press and hold the **Home** *button to activate Siri.*

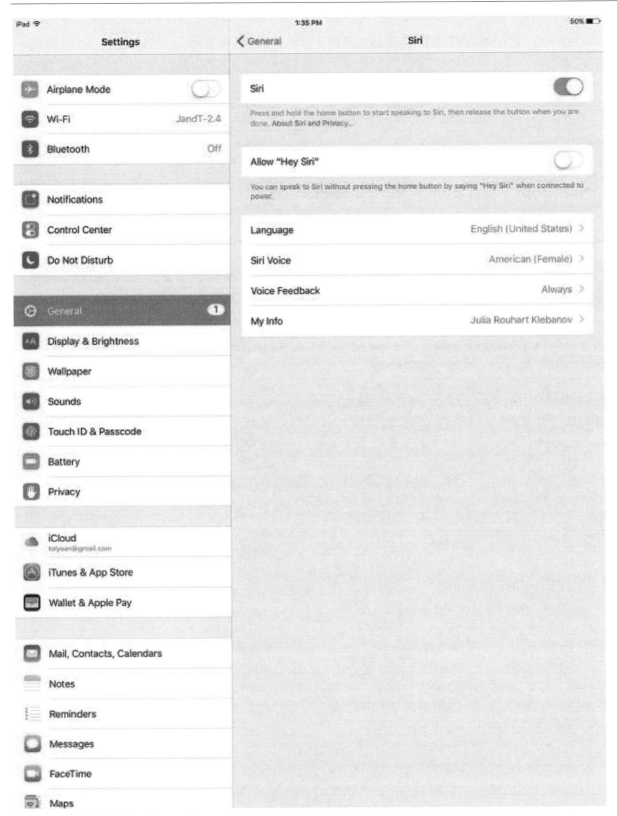

Figure 10: Siri Settings Screen

6. Changing the Keyboard Layout

The layout of the keyboard in most languages can be changed, according to personal preference. For instance, the English keyboard can be set display in default QWERTY, as shown in **Figure 11**, AZERTY, as shown in **Figure 12**, or QWERTZ as shown in **Figure 13**. To change the Keyboard Layout:

1. Touch the ⊚ icon. The Settings screen appears.
2. Touch **General**. The General Settings screen appears.
3. Scroll down and touch **Keyboard**. The Keyboard Settings screen appears.
4. Touch **Keyboards**. The Keyboards screen appears.
5. Touch the language of the keyboard that you wish to change. The Keyboard Layout screen appears.
6. Touch the desired layout. The new Keyboard Layout is set.

Note: The English keyboard layouts are shown below only as an example. The keyboard layouts vary based on the language that you select.

Figure 11: QWERTY Keyboard

Figure 12: AZERTY Keyboard

Figure 13: QWERTZ Keyboard

7. Changing the Region Format

The region format on the iPad determines how dates, times, and phone numbers are universally displayed. For instance, a European country may display the 30th day of the first month in the year 2011 as 30/01/2011, whereas the U.S. would display the same date as 01/30/2011. To change the region format:

1. Touch the icon. The Settings screen appears.
2. Touch **General**. The General Settings screen appears.
3. Scroll down and touch **Language & Region**. The Language & Region screen appears.
4. Touch **Region**. A list of regions appears, as shown in **Figure 14**.
5. Touch the desired region. The new region format is set.

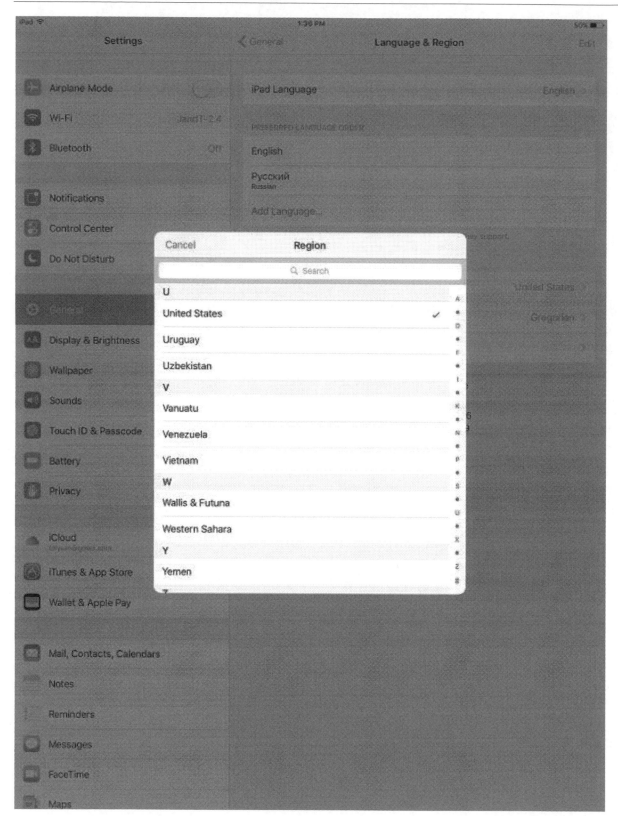

Figure 14: List of Regions

Adjusting General Settings

Table of Contents

1. Changing Auto-Lock Settings

The iPad can lock itself when it is idle in order to save battery life, and to avoid unintentionally pressing buttons. When it is locked, the iPad can still receive calls and text messages. By default, the iPad is set to automatically lock after one minute. To change the length of time that will pass before the iPad locks itself:

1. Touch the ⚙ icon. The Settings screen appears, as shown in **Figure 1**.
2. Touch **General**. The General Settings screen appears, as shown in **Figure 2**.
3. Scroll down and touch **Auto-Lock**. The Auto-Lock Settings screen appears, as shown in **Figure 3**.
4. Touch an amount of time, or touch **Never** if you do not want the iPad to automatically lock itself. The change is applied, and the iPad will wait the selected amount of time before automatically locking itself.

Figure 1: Settings Screen

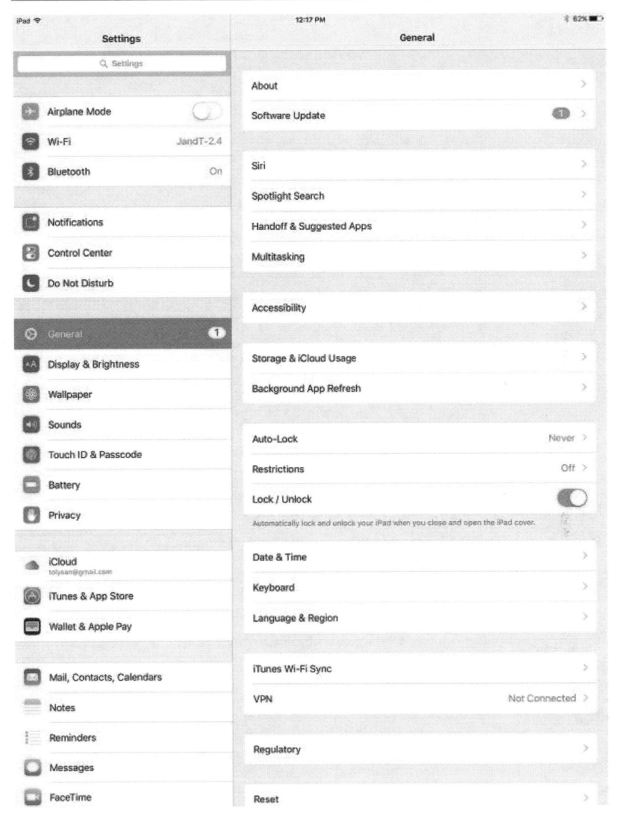

Figure 2: General Settings Screen

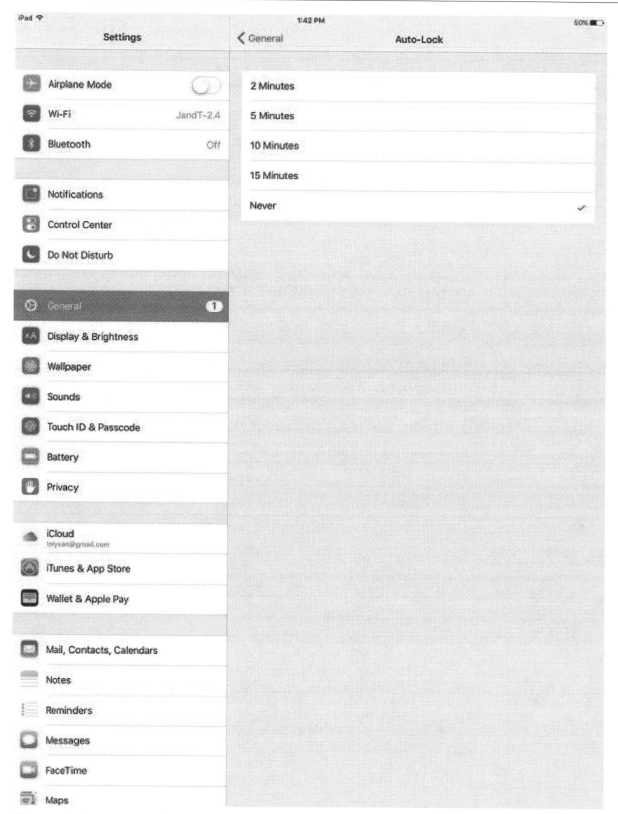

Figure 3: Auto-Lock Settings Screen

2. Adjusting the Brightness

You may wish to increase the brightness of the screen on your iPad when you are in a sunny area. On the other hand, you may wish to decrease the brightness in a dark area to conserve battery life. You can also turn Auto-Brightness on or off, which will determine whether or not the iPad automatically sets the brightness based on the lighting conditions. To adjust the brightness:

1. Touch the ⚙ icon. The Settings screen appears.
2. Touch **Display & Brightness**. The Display & Brightness Settings screen appears, as shown in **Figure 4**.
3. Touch the ⚪ on the ▬▬▬▬⚪ bar and drag it towards the small ☀ icon to decrease the brightness or towards the large ☀ icon to increase it.
4. Touch the ⬤○ switch next to 'Auto-Brightness' to disable Auto-Brightness, or touch the ○⬤ switch to enable it. Auto-Brightness it turned off or on, respectively.

Note: While Auto-Brightness is enabled, you can still temporarily adjust the brightness of the screen. However, as soon as the lighting conditions change, the iPad will automatically change the brightness.

iPad 🌐	1:42 PM	50% ■□
Settings	**Display & Brightness**	

Airplane Mode

Wi-Fi   JandT-2.4

Bluetooth   Off

Notifications

Control Center

Do Not Disturb

General ①

Display & Brightness

Wallpaper

Sounds

Touch ID & Passcode

Battery

Privacy

iCloud
tolysen@gmail.com

iTunes & App Store

Wallet & Apple Pay

Mail, Contacts, Calendars

Notes

Reminders

Messages

FaceTime

Maps

BRIGHTNESS

☀   ☀

Auto-Brightness

Night Shift   10:00 PM to 7:00 AM >

DISPLAY ZOOM

View   Standard >

Choose a view for iPad. Zoomed shows larger controls. Standard shows more content.

Text Size   >

Bold Text

Figure 4: Display & Brightness Settings Screen

3. Assigning a Passcode Lock or Fingerprint Lock

The iPad can prompt for a four-digit or alphanumeric password, or your fingerprint before unlocking.

To set up a password lock:

1. Touch the ⚙ icon. The Settings screen appears.
2. Touch **Touch ID & Passcode**. The Touch ID & Passcode screen appears, as shown in **Figure 5**.
3. Touch **Turn Passcode On**. The Set Passcode screen appears, as shown in **Figure 6**, where you can enter a numeric passcode. To enter an alphanumeric password instead, touch **Passcode Options**, and then touch **Custom Alphanumeric Code**. The Set Password screen appears, as shown in **Figure 7**.
4. Enter a passcode. A confirmation screen appears.
5. Enter the passcode again. The new passcode is set.
6. Touch one of the following options on the Passcode Lock screen to change the corresponding setting:
   - **Require Passcode** - Set the time the iPad waits before asking the user for the passcode. It is recommended to choose the default, **Immediately**, since an unauthorized user will not have access to your iPad for any period of time if this option is chosen. Choosing one of the other options causes the iPad to wait a set amount of time after being locked before requiring a passcode.
   - **Erase Data** - Erases all data after a user enters the passcode incorrectly ten times in a row.

Warning: You will not be able to recover your data if the Erase Data feature is on when an incorrect passcode is entered ten times consecutively.

To set up a fingerprint lock:

1. Set up a password lock. Refer to the instructions above to learn how.
2. Touch **Add a fingerprint**. The Touch ID screen appears.
3. Touch (do not press) the Home button with the finger that you want to use to unlock the iPad.
4. Lift and rest your finger on the Home button repeatedly. Keep doing this until the Fingerprint Confirmation screen appears, as shown in **Figure 8**. Your fingerprint can now be used to unlock the iPad. To unlock the iPad, activate the screen and scan your fingerprint.

Figure 5: Touch ID & Passcode Screen

Figure 6: Set Passcode Screen

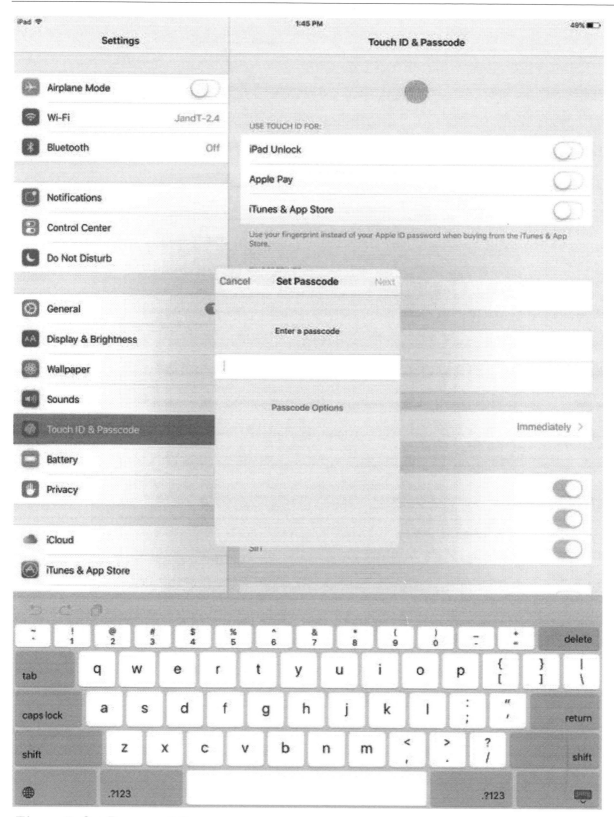

Figure 7: Set Password Screen

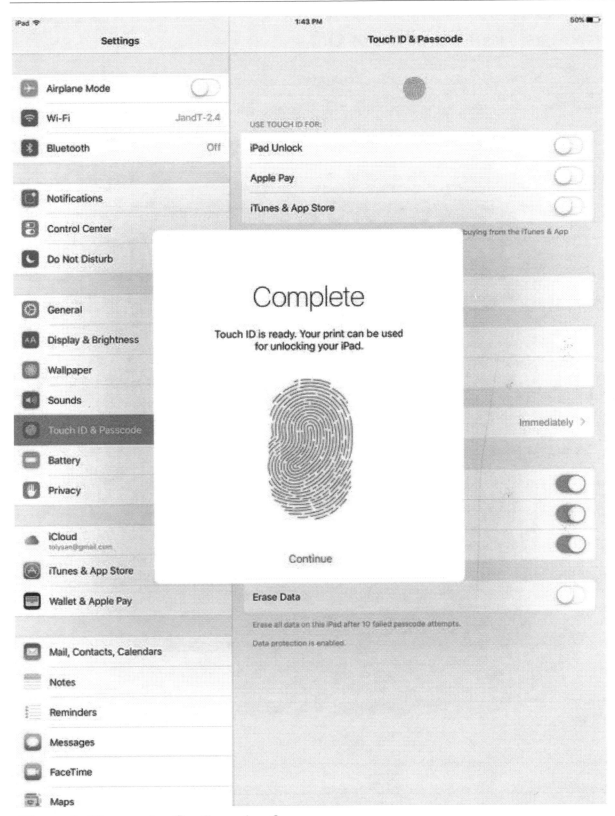

Figure 8: Fingerprint Confirmation Screen

4. Turning 24-Hour Mode On or Off

The iPad can display the time in regular 12-hour mode or in 24-hour mode, commonly referred to as military time. To turn 24-hour mode on or off:

1. Touch the ⚙ icon. The Settings screen appears.
2. Touch **General**. The General Settings screen appears.
3. Scroll down and touch **Date & Time**. The Date & Time screen appears, as shown in **Figure 9**.

4. Touch the ⬭ switch next to '24-Hour Time'. The ⬤ switch appears 24-Hour mode is turned on.

5. Touch the ⬤ switch next to '24-Hour Time'. The ⬭ switch appears and 24-Hour mode is turned off.

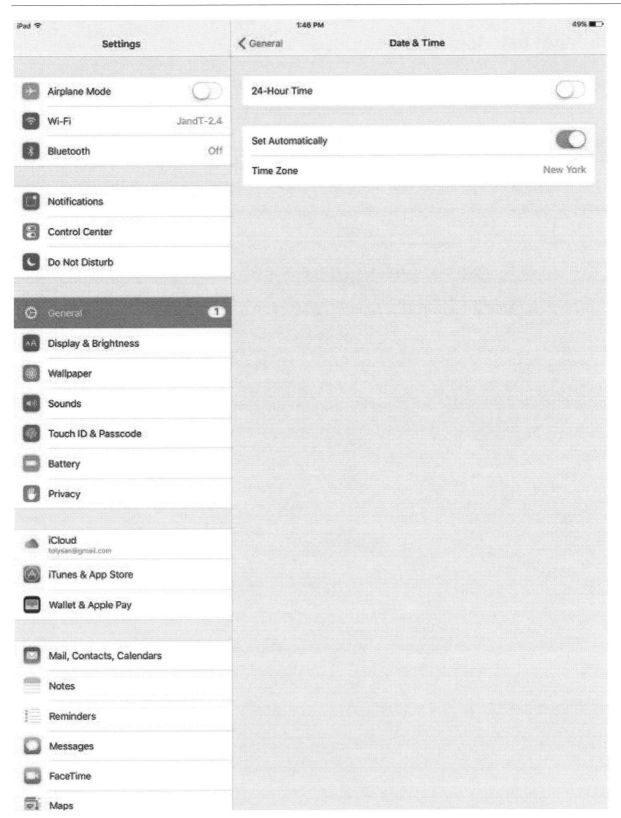

Figure 9: Date & Time Screen

5. Resetting the Home Screen Layout

You can reset the Home screen on your iPad to look like it did when you first purchased it. To reset the Home Screen Layout:

Note: Resetting the Home screen layout does not delete any applications, but simply rearranges them on the Home screen.

1. Touch the [icon] icon. The Settings screen appears.
2. Touch **General**. The General Settings screen appears.
3. Scroll down and touch **Reset**. The Reset screen appears, as shown in **Figure 10**.
4. Touch **Reset Home Screen Layout**. A confirmation dialog appears at the bottom of the screen.
5. Touch **Reset Home Screen**. The Home Screen Layout is reset.

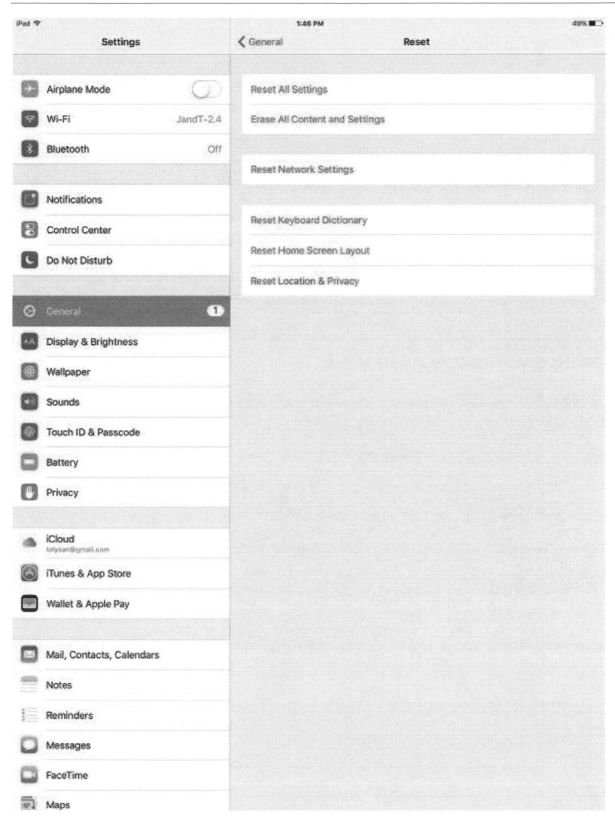

Figure 10: Reset Screen

6. Resetting All Settings

You can reset all of the settings on your iPad to the state they were in when you first purchased it. To reset all settings:

Note: Resetting the settings will NOT delete any data from your iPad.

1. Touch the ![icon] icon. The Settings screen appears.
2. Touch **General**. The General Settings screen appears.
3. Scroll down and touch **Reset**. The Reset screen appears.
4. Touch **Reset All Settings**. A confirmation dialog appears at the bottom of the screen. You will also need to enter your passcode, if you have one.
5. Touch **Reset All Settings**. All settings are reset to defaults.

7. Erasing and Restoring the iPad

You can delete all of the data and reset all settings to completely restore the iPad to its original condition. To erase and restore the iPad to its original condition:

Warning: Any erased data is not recoverable. Make sure that you back up all of the data that you wish to keep.

1. Touch the ![icon] icon. The Settings screen appears.
2. Touch **General**. The General Settings screen appears.
3. Touch **Reset**. The Reset screen appears.
4. Touch **Erase All Content and Settings**. A confirmation appears at the bottom of the screen.
5. Touch **Erase**. The iPad is erased and restored to its original condition.

8. Managing Notification Settings

You may customize the types of notifications that appear in the Notifications Center. To manage notification settings:

1. Touch the [icon] icon. The Settings screen appears.
2. Touch **Notifications**. The Notifications Settings appear, as shown in **Figure 11**.
3. Touch one of the notification types, such as Messages or Reminders, to turn the notifications on or off, or to customize the number of notifications that appear. The Notification Customization screen, as shown in **Figure 12** (Message Notification Customization).
4. Touch the [switch] switch next to 'Allow Notifications'. The [switch] switch appears and notifications will no longer appear for the selected type.
5. Touch one of the following options to customize the notifications:

Note: The following options will vary based on the notification type:

- **Show in Notification Center** - Select the number of recent items that should appear in the Notifications Center for the selected type.
- **Notification Sound** - Select the sound that plays when a new notification of the selected type arrives.
- **Badge App Icon** - Turn the notification type icon that appears next to a notification on or off.
- **Show on Lock Screen** - Allow notifications of the selected type to appear on the Lock screen.
- **Alert Style When Unlocked** - Touch **None**, **Banners**, or **Alerts** to select the way in which notifications appear for the selected type.

Figure 11: Notifications Settings

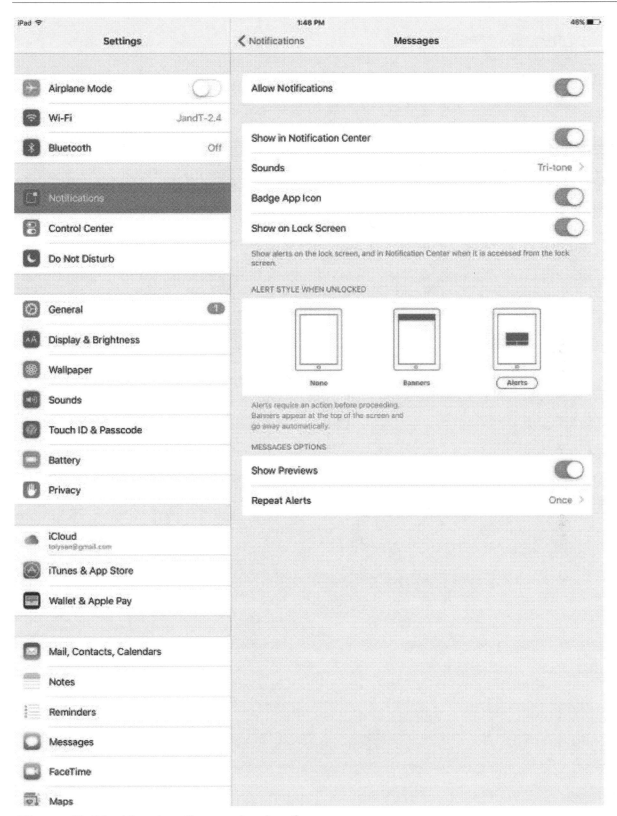

Figure 12: Notification Customization Screen

9. Changing the Wallpaper

The wallpaper is the image that appears on the Lock screen, and on the Home screen behind the application icons. To change the wallpaper:

1. Touch the ⦿ icon. The Settings screen appears.
2. Touch **Wallpaper**. The Wallpaper Settings appear, as shown in **Figure 13**.
3. Touch **Choose a New Wallpaper**. The Wallpaper Selection screen appears, as shown in **Figure 14**.
4. Touch the image above 'Dynamic' or 'Stills', or touch one of the photo albums under 'Photos'. The corresponding image thumbnails appear.
5. Touch an image thumbnail. The image appears in full-screen, as shown in **Figure 15**.
6. Touch **Set Lock Screen**, **Set Home Screen**, or **Set Both** to set the corresponding wallpaper. The new wallpaper is set. Alternatively, touch **Cancel** to select another image.

iPad 📶   1:48 PM   48% 🔋

Settings	Wallpaper

WALLPAPER

Choose a New Wallpaper   >

Airplane Mode ⬜

Wi-Fi   JandT-2.4

Bluetooth   Off

Notifications

Control Center

Do Not Disturb

General 🔘

Display & Brightness

Wallpaper

Sounds

Touch ID & Passcode

Battery

Privacy

iCloud
tolysan@gmail.com

iTunes & App Store

Wallet & Apple Pay

Mail, Contacts, Calendars

Notes

Reminders

Messages

FaceTime

Maps

Figure 13: Wallpaper Settings

Figure 14: Wallpaper Selection

Figure 15: Wallpaper Image in Full-Screen

10. Restricting Access to Private Information

Some applications may request to use your some of the information stored on your iPad, or even to access your camera. If you touch **Allow**, the application will have access to the requested information until you take away the access. To restrict access to private information:

1. Touch the ⊙ icon. The Settings screen appears.
2. Touch **Privacy**. The Privacy Settings screen appears, as shown in **Figure 16**.
3. Touch one of the information types, such as 'Contacts' or 'Calendars'. The list of applications appear that have requested access to the selected type of information, as shown in **Figure 17** (Contacts).

4. Touch the ⬤ switch next to the name of the requesting application. The ◯ switch appears, and the selected application will no longer have access to the type of information selected in step 3.

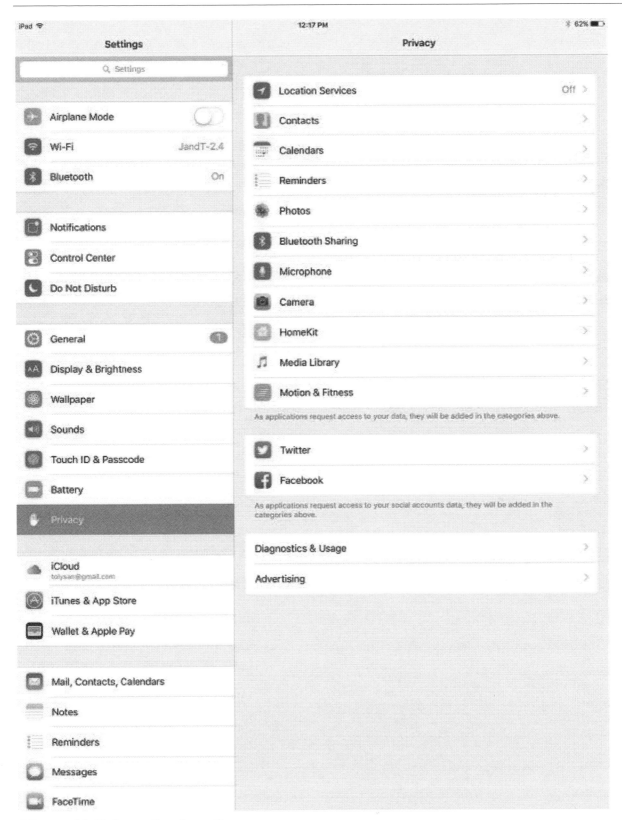

Figure 16: Privacy Settings Screen

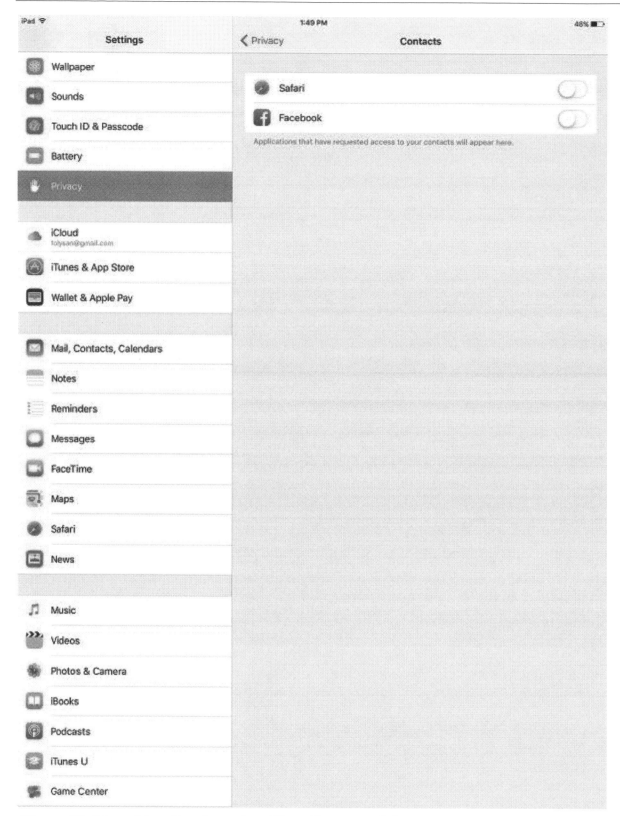

Figure 17: List of Applications that Have Requested Access

Adjusting Accessibility Settings

Table of Contents

1. Managing Vision Accessibility Features

Vision accessibility features allow people with visual disabilities to use the iPad with greater ease. To manage vision accessibility features:

1. Touch the ![icon] icon. The Settings screen appears, as shown in **Figure 1**.
2. Touch **General**. The General Settings screen appears, as shown in **Figure 2**.
3. Touch **Accessibility**. The Accessibility Settings screen appears, as shown in **Figure 3**.
4. Touch one of the following options to turn vision accessibility features on or off:

   - **VoiceOver** - This feature speaks an item on the screen when you touch it once, activates it when you touch it twice, and scrolls through a list or page of text when you touch the screen with three fingers.
   - **Zoom** - This features zooms in on an item when you touch the screen twice using three fingers, moves around when you drag three fingers on the screen, and changes the level of zoom when you touch the screen with three fingers twice and drag.
   - **Invert Colors** - This feature inverts all of the colors on the screen. For instance, black text on a white screen becomes white text on a black screen.
   - **Grayscale** - This feature changes all color on the iPad's screen to black and white.
   - **Larger Text** - This feature increases the default size of the font. Use the font slider to adjust the default font size.
   - **Bold Text** - This feature makes all text on the iPad bold in order to make it easier to read. Enabling or disabling this feature requires you to restart the iPad.
   - **Button Shapes** - This feature allows all buttons, such as the back button in the upper left-hand corner of each menu screen, to have outlines.
   - **Increase Contrast** - This feature improves the contrast on certain backgrounds in order to make it easier to read certain text.

- **Reduce Motion** - This feature turns off all screen animations, such as when you close an application to return to the Home screen.

- **On/Off Labels** - This feature turns [switch] and [switch] switches into [switch] and [switch] switches, respectively.

Touch **Speech** to turn one of the following settings on or off:

- **Speak Selection** - This feature allows all text on the screen to be spoken aloud when you select it and touch **Speak**.
- **Speak Screen** - This feature allows all the contents of the screen to be described when you touch the top of the screen with two fingers and slide down.
- **Speak Auto-text** - This feature speaks every auto-correction or auto-capitalization as you enter text in any text field, including text messages and emails.

Figure 1: Settings Screen

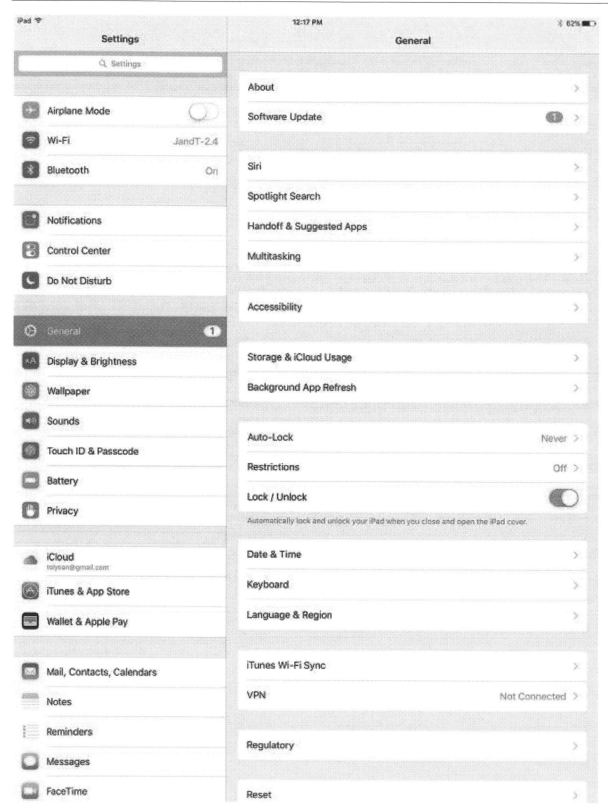

Figure 2: General Settings Screen

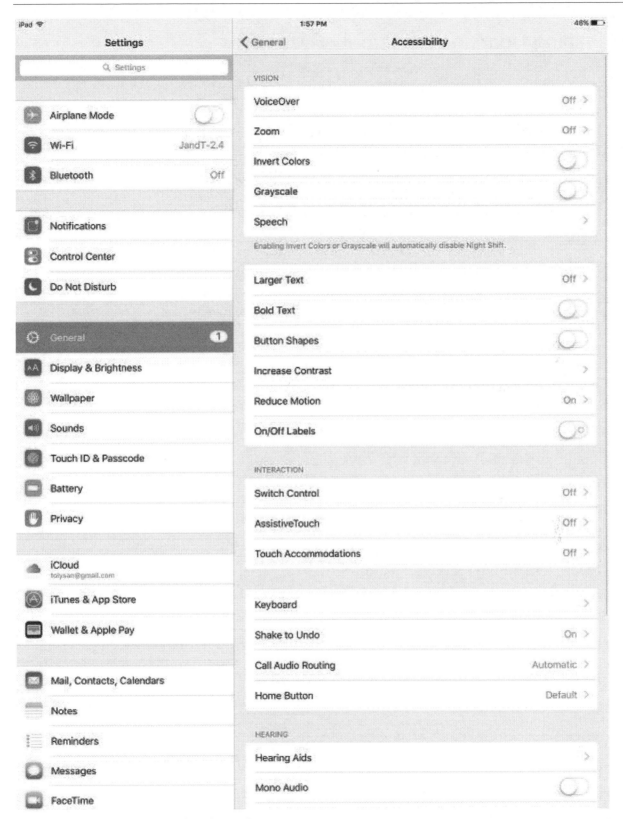

Figure 3: Accessibility Settings Screen

2. Managing Hearing Accessibility Features

Hearing accessibility features allow people with hearing disabilities to use the iPad with greater ease. To manage hearing accessibility features:

1. Touch the [icon] icon. The Settings screen appears.
2. Touch **General**. The General Settings screen appears.
3. Touch **Accessibility**. The Accessibility Settings screen appears.
4. Touch one of the following options to turn hearing accessibility features on or off:
   - **Hearing Aids** - This feature automatically manages the antenna in the iPad to avoid interference with standard hearing aids and improve overall performance. However, cellular reception may be reduced when using this feature.
   - **Subtitles & Captioning** - This feature allows subtitles and closed captioning to be enabled for videos, where available.
   - **Mono Audio** - This feature turns off stereo audio, leaving only one speaker working.

3. Turning Guided Access On or Off

Guided Access is a feature that is made for people with learning disabilities, allowing the user to stay in a single application and control the features that are available. To turn Guided Access on or off:

1. Touch the [icon] icon. The Settings screen appears.
2. Touch **General**. The General Settings screen appears.
3. Touch **Accessibility**. The Accessibility Settings screen appears.
4. Scroll down and touch **Guided Access**. The Guided Access Settings screen appears, as shown in **Figure 4**.
5. Touch the [switch] switch next to 'Guided Access'. Guided Access is turned on.
6. Touch **Set Passcode** to set up a passcode that will allow you to exit the application when you are done using it.

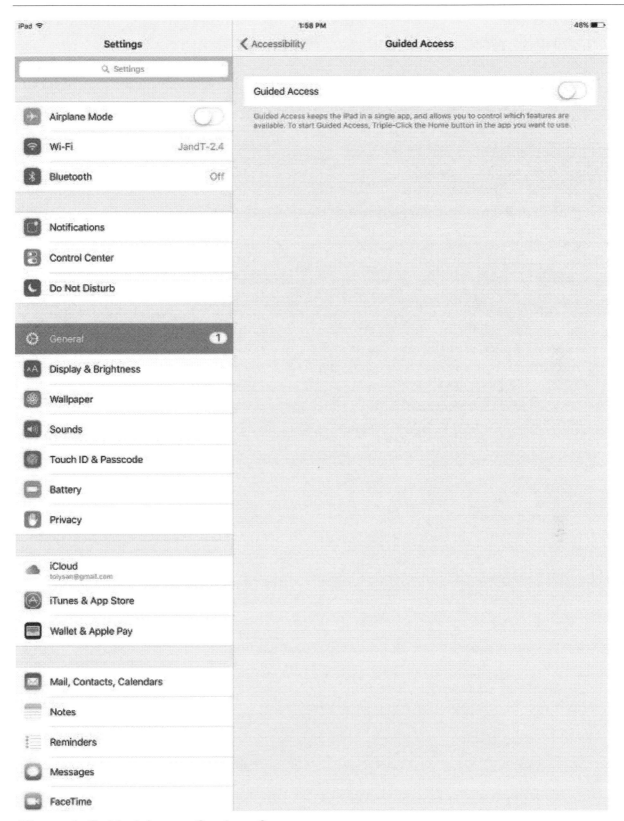

Figure 4: Guided Access Settings Screen

4. Managing Physical & Motor Accessibility Features

Physical and Motor accessibility features allow people with motor disabilities to use the iPad with greater ease. To manage physical & motor accessibility features:

1. Touch the ⚙ icon. The Settings screen appears.
2. Touch **General**. The General Settings screen appears.
3. Touch **Accessibility**. The Accessibility Settings screen appears.
4. Touch one of the following options to turn physical and motor accessibility features on or off:
   - **Switch Control** - This feature allows an adaptive accessory to be used to highlight items on the screen to control the functions of the iPad. The Switch Control screen allows various settings, such as timing, switch stabilization, point scanning, audio, and visual settings, to be adjusted.
   - **Assistive Touch** - This feature allows you to create custom gestures in order to access various services on the iPad.
   - **Home-click Speed** - This feature allows you to slow down the speed at which you need to press the Home button to access certain features.
   - **Accessibility Shortcut** - This feature allows you to select an accessibility feature that will be turned on when you press the Home button three times quickly at any time. If you choose more than one feature, a menu will appear allowing you to select the Accessibility feature that you wish to enable.

Adjusting Text Message Settings

Table of Contents

1. Turning iMessage On or Off

The iMessage feature allows you to send free text messages to other iPads, as well as iPhones and iPod Touch devices. Turn on iMessage to send a message using the email address assigned to the recipient's iMessage account. By default, iMessage is turned on. It is not possible to send a message to a person using an Android device, since Android does not support iMessage. To turn iMessage on or off:

1. Touch the icon. The Settings screen appears, as shown in **Figure 1**.
2. Scroll down and touch **Messages**. The Message Settings screen appears, as shown in **Figure 2**.
3. Touch the switch next to 'iMessage'. The switch appears and iMessage is turned on.
4. Touch the switch next to 'iMessage'. The switch appears and iMessage is turned off.

Figure 1: Settings Screen

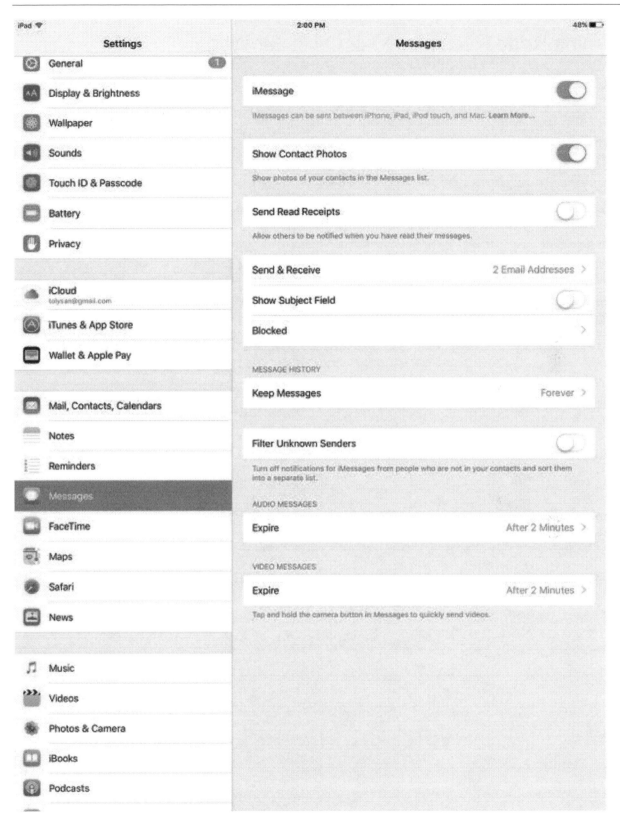

Figure 2: Message Settings Screen

2. Turning Read Receipts On or Off in iMessage

After receiving and opening a message from an iPhone, iPad, or iPod Touch, your iPad can notify the sender that you have opened and read the message. These notifications are called Read Receipts, and appear under the original message on the sender's screen as "Read", followed by a time. Read Receipts are only compatible with the three Apple iPads listed above. To turn Read Receipts on or off:

1. Touch the ⚙ icon. The Settings screen appears.
2. Scroll down and touch **Messages**. The Message Settings screen appears.
3. Touch the ⬜ switch next to 'Send Read Receipts'. The 🔘 switch appears and Read Receipts are turned on.
4. Touch the 🔘 switch next to 'Send Read Receipts'. The ⬜ switch appears and Read Receipts are turned off.

3. Turning the Subject Field On or Off

The iPad can attach a subject to each text message it sends when the subject field is enabled. The subject appears in parentheses preceding the message content. To turn the subject field on or off:

1. Touch the ⚙ icon. The Settings screen appears.
2. Scroll down and touch **Messages**. The Message Settings screen appears.
3. Touch the ⬜ switch next to 'Show Subject Field'. The 🔘 switch appears and the Subject field is turned on.
4. Touch the 🔘 switch next to 'Show Subject Field'. The ⬜ switch appears and the Subject field is turned off.

4. Setting the Amount of Time to Keep Messages

When using iMessage, text messages can be automatically deleted after a certain period of time. To set the amount of time to keep messages:

1. Touch the ⚙ icon. The Settings screen appears.
2. Scroll down and touch **Messages**. The Message Settings screen appears.
3. Touch **Keep Messages**. The Keep Messages screen appears, as shown in **Figure 3**.
4. Touch **30 Days** or **1 Year** to select the amount of time, or touch **Forever** to prevent the iPad from erasing any messages.

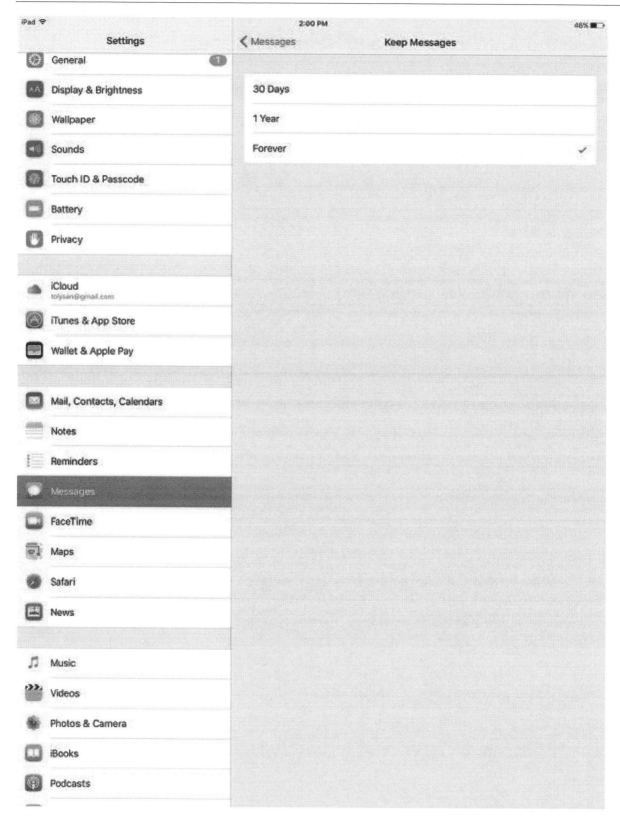

Figure 3: Keep Messages Screen

5. Setting the Expiration Time for Audio Messages

When an audio message is sent using iMessage, it can be set to expire after two minutes, at which point it is removed from your iPad. Refer to *"Adding a Voice Message to a Conversation"* on page 73 to learn how to attach audio messages in iMessage. To set the expiration time for audio messages:

1. Touch the ⚙ icon. The Settings screen appears.
2. Scroll down and touch **Messages**. The Message Settings screen appears.
3. Touch **Expire** under 'Audio Messages'. The Audio Message Expiration screen appears, as shown in **Figure 4**.
4. Touch **After 2 Minutes**, or touch **Never** to keep audio messages.

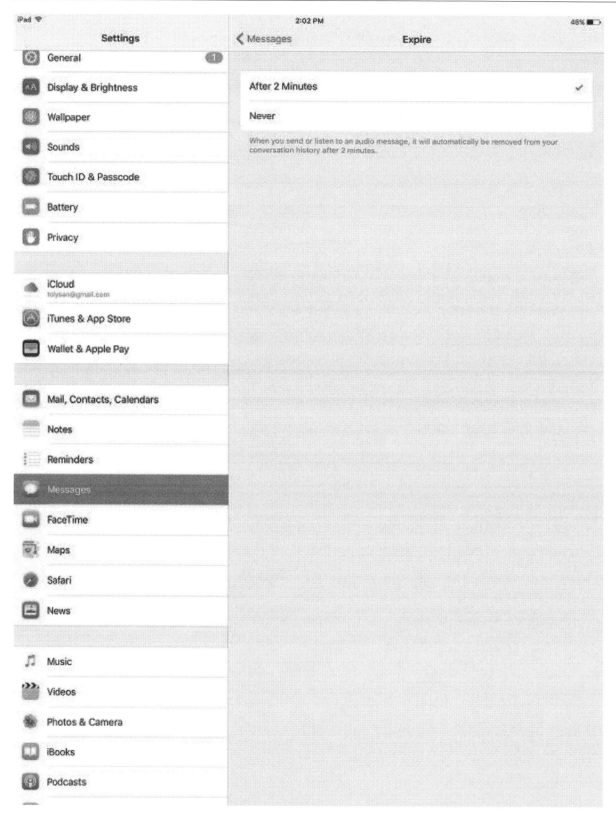

Figure 4: Audio Message Expiration Screen

6. Setting the Expiration Time for Video Messages

When a video message is sent using iMessage, it can be set to expire after two minutes, at which point it is removed from your iPad. Refer to *"Quickly Adding a Video or Photo to a Conversation (iMessage Only)"* on page 75 to learn how to attach video messages in iMessage. To set the expiration time for video messages:

1. Touch the icon. The Settings screen appears.
2. Scroll down and touch **Messages**. The Message Settings screen appears.
3. Touch **Expire** under 'Video Messages'. The Video Message Expiration screen appears.
4. Touch **After 2 Minutes**, or touch **Never** to keep video messages.

Adjusting Music Application Settings

Table of Contents

1. Selecting a Pre-Loaded Equalization Setting

The iPad has several custom, pre-loaded Equalization settings that can be applied in order to improve the sound of your music. To select an Equalization setting:

Note: In order to quickly select the optimal EQ setting for you, turn on some music before performing the steps below. Refer to "Using the Music Application" *on page 131 to learn how.*

1. Touch the ⊚ icon. The Settings screen appears, as shown in **Figure 1**.
2. Scroll down and touch **Music**. The Music Settings screen appears, as shown in **Figure 2**.
3. Touch **EQ**. A list of EQ settings appears, as shown in **Figure 3**.
4. Touch an EQ setting. The EQ setting is applied to all music that plays via the Music application.
5. Touch **Music** at the top of the screen. The EQ setting is saved.

Figure 1: Settings Screen

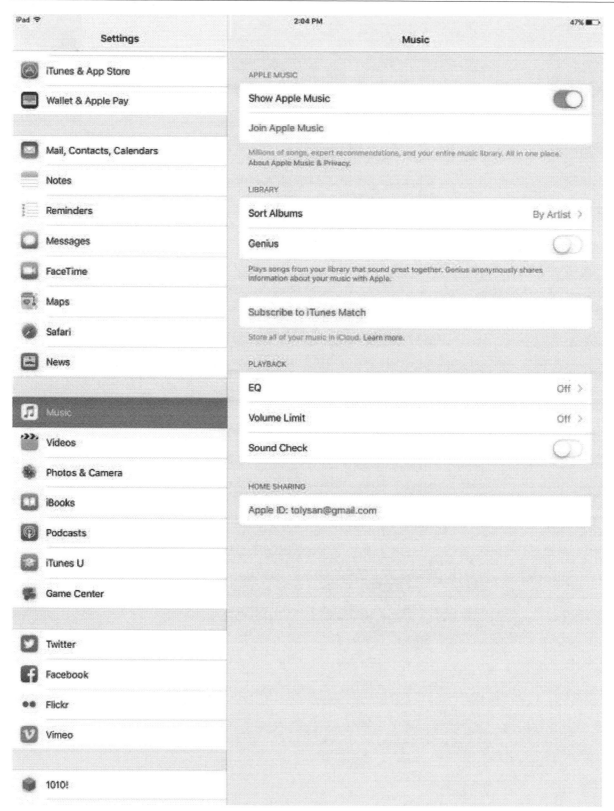

Figure 2: Music Settings Screen

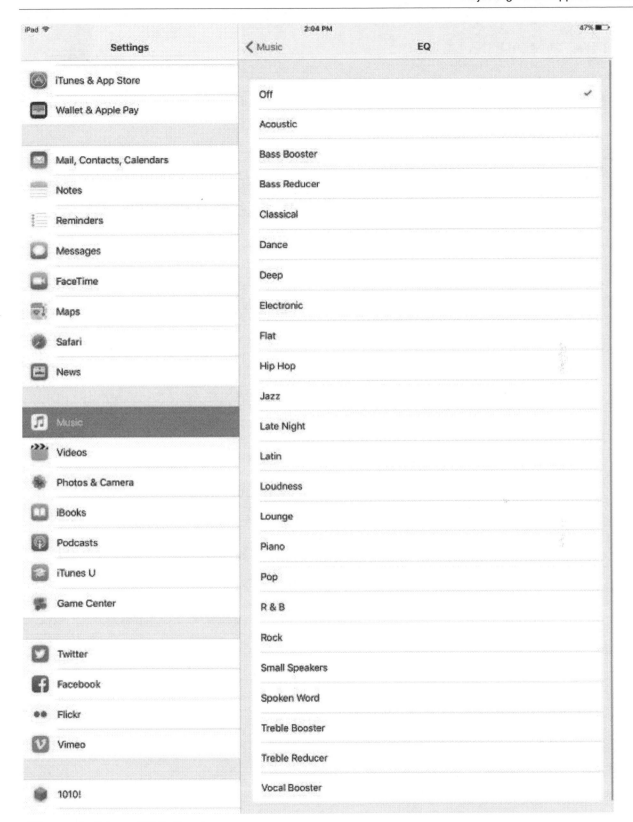

Figure 3: List of EQ Settings

2. Setting a Volume Limit

In order to prevent increasing the volume in the Music application by accidentally pressing the volume buttons, try setting a Volume Limit. To set a Volume Limit:

1. Touch the icon. The Settings screen appears.
2. Scroll down and touch **Music**. The Music Settings screen appears.
3. Touch **Volume Limit**. The Volume Limit screen appears, as shown in **Figure 4**.
4. Touch the on the bar, and drag it to the desired location. The new volume limit is selected.
5. Touch **Music** at the top of the screen. The Volume Limit is saved.

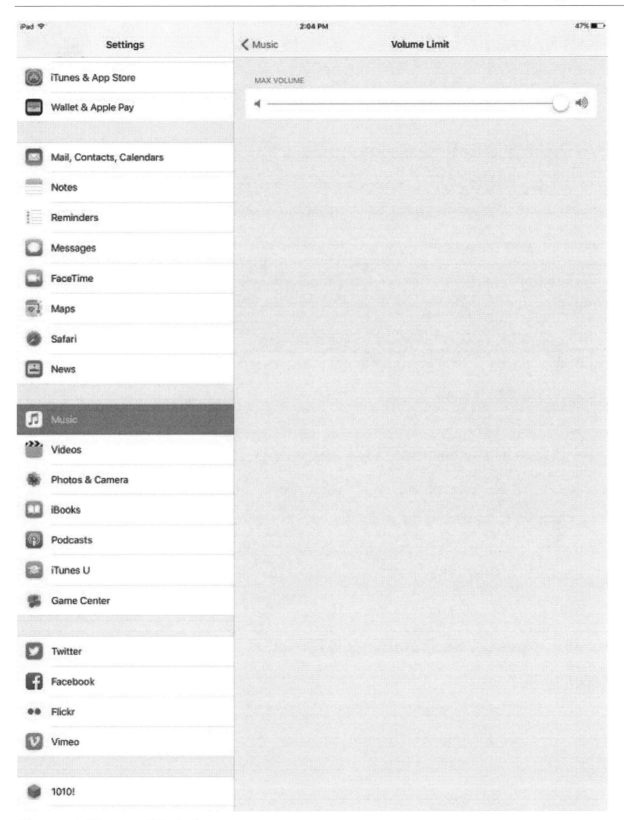

Figure 4: Volume Limit Screen

3. Choosing which Music Appears in the Music Application

The Music application can either display all of your music, both in the Cloud and on your iPad, or just the music on your iPad. To choose which music appears in the music application:

1. Touch the icon. The Settings screen appears.
2. Scroll down and touch **Music**. The Music Settings screen appears.
3. Touch the switch next to 'Show All Music'. The switch appears and both music on your iPad and in the Cloud will be shown in the Music application.
4. Touch the switch next to 'Show All Music'. The switch appears and only the music on your iPad will be shown in the Music application.

4. Turning iTunes Match On or Off

iTunes Match is a service that Apple offers at $24.99 per year, which allows you to play songs from Apple's Cloud at the highest quality, as long as the song already exists in your library. iTunes Match songs can be played on any one of your registered iPads. To use iTunes Match, you must first subscribe by touching **Subscribe to iTunes Match** on the Music Settings screen. You may need to enter your Apple credentials. To turn iTunes Match on or off on the iPad:

1. Touch the icon. The Settings screen appears.
2. Scroll down and touch **Music**. The Music Settings screen appears.
3. Touch the switch next to 'iTunes Match'. The Password prompt appears.
4. Enter your Apple credentials and touch **OK**. The switch appears and iTunes Match is turned on.
5. Touch the switch next to 'iTunes Match'. The switch appears and iTunes Match is turned off.

Adjusting Photo and Video Settings

Table of Contents

1. Turning Photo Stream On or Off

Photo Stream allows you to instantly load photos you have taken on your iPad to your other registered Apple iPads. It accomplishes this by automatically uploading them to the iCloud and then downloading them to other Apple devices that are registered under the same Apple ID. To turn Photo Stream on or off:

1. Touch the ⚙ icon. The Settings screen appears, as shown in **Figure 1**.
2. Scroll down and touch **Photos & Camera**. The Photo Settings screen appears, as shown in **Figure 2**.

3. Touch the ⬜ switch next to 'Upload to My Photo Stream'. The ⬛ switch appears and Photo Stream is turned on.

4. Touch the ⬛ switch next to 'Upload to My Photo Stream'. The ⬜ switch appears and Photo Stream is turned off.

Note: You can also touch the ⬜ switch next to iCloud Photo Library to upload your photos and videos to iCloud for safekeeping.

Figure 1: Settings Screen

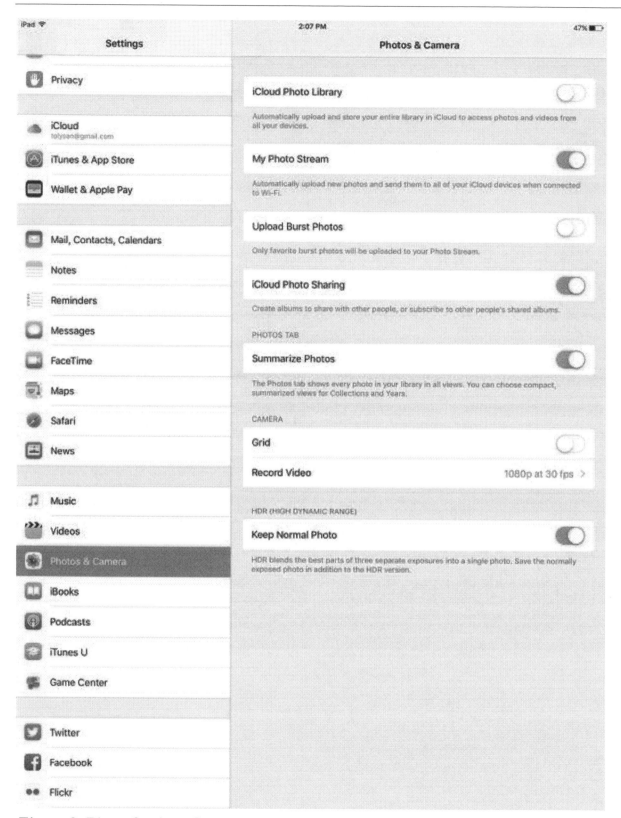

Figure 2: Photo Settings Screen

2. Customizing High Dynamic Range (HDR) Camera Settings

When taking photos with the iPad, you can enable HDR, which will improve picture quality by taking several photos, and average the light levels for a much more realistic photo. To turn on HDR, touch **HDR Off** at the top of the screen while the camera is running. When HDR is turned on, a non-HDR copy of each photo is stored by default. To customize HDR settings:

1. Touch the ⚙ icon. The Settings screen appears.
2. Scroll down and touch **Photos and Camera**. The Photo Settings screen appears.
3. Touch the ⚪ switch next to 'Keep Normal Photo'. The ⚪ switch appears and the iPad will now delete non-HDR photos while keeping the HDR copy.
4. Touch the ⚪ switch next to 'Keep Normal Photo'. The ⚫ switch appears and the iPad will keep the non-HDR photo in addition to the HDR copy when taking photos.

Note: An HDR photo takes up more memory on your iPad than a non-HDR one.

3. Customizing Video Playback Settings

After a video is stopped (not paused), the iPad can resume playing it from the beginning or from where you last left off. To customize Video Playback settings:

1. Touch the ⚙ icon. The Settings screen appears.
2. Scroll down and touch **Videos**. The Video Settings screen appears, as shown in **Figure 3**.
3. Touch **Start Playing**. The Start Playing screen appears, as shown in **Figure 4**.
4. Touch **From Beginning**. Videos will now resume from the beginning.
5. Touch **Where Left Off**. Videos will now resume where they last left off.
6. Touch **Videos** at the top of the screen. Your video playback selection is saved.

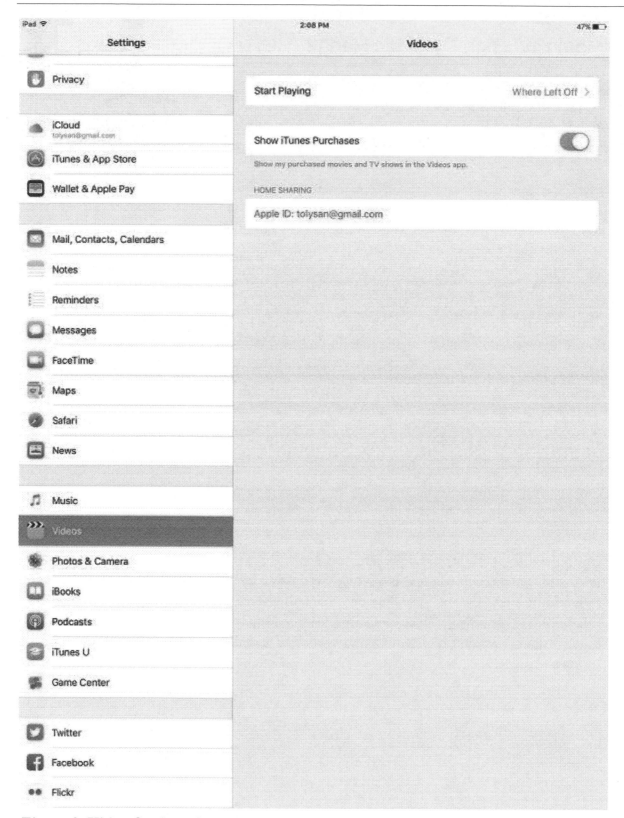

Figure 3: Video Settings Screen

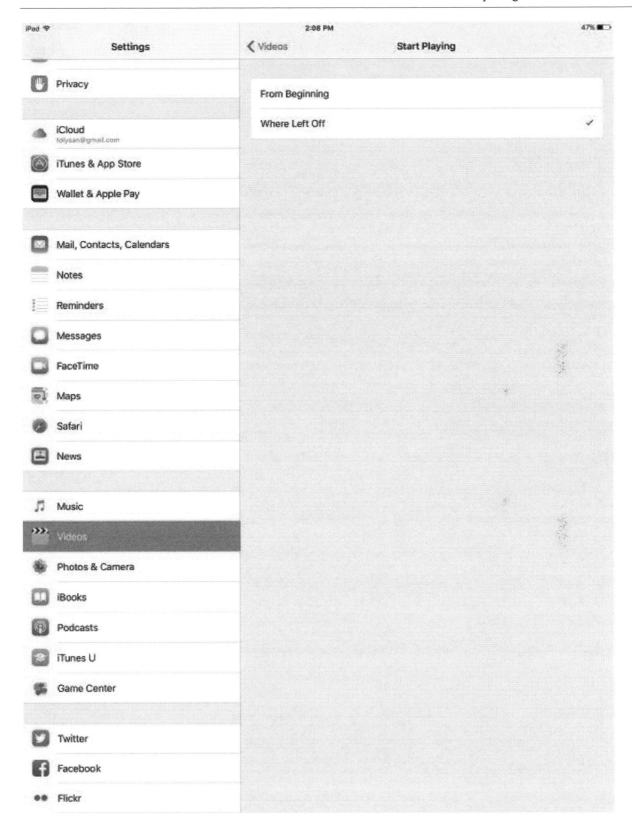

Figure 4: Start Playing Screen

4. Choosing which Videos Appear in the Videos Application

The Music application can either display all of your videos, both those that you purchased and ones that you imported from your computer, or just those that you imported. To choose which videos appear in the Videos application:

1. Touch the icon. The Settings screen appears.
2. Scroll down and touch **Videos**. The Video Settings screen appears.

3. Touch the ⬜ switch next to 'Show iTunes Purchases'. The ⬛ switch appears and all videos, both on your iPad and in the Cloud will appear in the Videos application.

4. Touch the ⬛ switch next to 'Show iTunes Purchases'. The ⬜ switch appears and only videos on your iPad will appear in the Videos application.

Tips and Tricks

Table of Contents

1. Maximizing Battery Life

There are several things you can do to increase the battery life of the iPad.

- Lock the iPad whenever you are not using it. To lock the iPad, press the **Sleep/Wake** button at the top of the iPad. Refer to *"Button Layout"* on page 9 for the location of the Sleep/Wake button.
- Keep the Auto-lock feature on and set it to a small amount of time. Refer to *"Changing Auto-Lock Settings"* on page 243 to learn how to change Auto-lock settings.
- Turn down the brightness and turn off Auto-Brightness. Refer to *"Adjusting the Brightness"* on page 247 to learn how.
- Turn on Airplane mode in areas where there is little or no signal, as the iPad will continually try to search for service. Refer to *"Turning Airplane Mode On or Off"* on page 204 to learn how to turn on Airplane Mode. This tip is iPad 4G only.
- Make sure to let the battery drain completely and then charge it fully at least once a month. This will help both short-term and long-term battery life.
- Turn off Wi-Fi when it is not in use. Refer to *"Using Wi-Fi"* on page 19 to learn how.
- Turn off Location Services when it is not in use. Refer to *"Turning Location Services On or Off"* on page 206 to learn how.
- Turn on the Grayscale accessibility feature. This will prevent you from seeing any colors, but is a great feature to use when your battery is running low. Refer to *"Managing Vision Accessibility Features"* on page 269 to learn how.

Refer to the tips below to learn more. In addition, you can view a list of applications that are using up most of your battery. To view battery usage:

1. Touch the ⚙ icon. The Settings screen appears.
2. Touch **General**. The General Settings screen appears.
3. Touch **Usage**. The Usage screen appears.
4. Touch **Battery Usage**. The Battery Usage screen appears, showing all of the applications that are draining your battery, and the percentage of the battery that each has drained. Refer to *"Closing an Application Running in the Background"* on page 184 to learn how to cut down on the amount of battery used by applications.

2. Taking a Screenshot

To capture what is on the screen and save it as a photo, press and hold the **Home** button, and then press the **Sleep/Wake** Button. Release the buttons and the screen will momentarily flash white. The screenshot is saved to the 'Recently Added' album.

3. Scrolling to the Top of a Screen

Touch anywhere in the notification bar at the very top of the screen to quickly scroll to the top of a list, website, etc. The notification bar is where the clock and battery meter are located.

4. Saving an Image While Browsing the Internet

To save an image from Safari to the iPad, touch and hold the picture until the Image menu appears. Touch **Save Image**. The image is saved to the 'Recently Added' album.

5. Inserting a Period

When typing a sentence, touch the space bar twice quickly to insert a period and a space.

6. Typing Alternate Characters

When typing a sentence, insert other characters, such as Á or Ñ, by touching and holding the base letter. A menu of characters appears above the letter. Slide your finger to a character to insert it.

7. Quickly Deleting Recently Typed Text

This feature is quite a secret. If you have just typed several lines of text and do not want any of it, just give the iPad a good shake. A menu appears asking whether to undo the typing. Touch **Undo**. The typed text is erased. Give the iPad another shake to redo the typing. This works in any application, or while text messaging.

8. Resetting the iPad

If the iPad or an application freezes up or is acting strangely, you may wish to reset the iPad. This will NOT wipe any data, but simply restart the operating system. To reset the iPad, hold the **Home** button and **Sleep/Wake** button together until the iPad completely shuts off. Continue to hold the buttons until the logo appears. The iPad resets and starts up.

9. Calling a Phone Number on a Website

You can call a phone number on a website directly. The number will be blue and underlined, much like a link. Touch the number. The iPad calls the number. If the number is on a website, the iPad will ask whether to call the number. Touch **Call**. This may not work with all websites.

10. Recovering Signal After Being in an Area with No Service (iPad 4G Only)

Sometimes the iPad has trouble finding signal after returning from an area where your network was not available. This issue can sometimes be fixed by turning Airplane Mode on and then back off. Refer to *"Turning Airplane Mode On or Off"* on page 204 to learn how.

11. Taking a Picture from the Lock Screen

To take a picture without unlocking the iPad, touch the icon and slide your finger up. The camera turns on. Press the **Volume Up** button. The camera takes a picture.

12. Assigning a Custom Ringtone to a Contact

You can assign a custom ringtone to any contact in the Phonebook. To assign a ringtone to a contact:

1. Touch the ![icon] icon. The Phonebook appears.
2. Find and touch the contact to whom you wish to assign a custom ringtone. The Contact Info screen appears. Refer to *"Finding a Contact"* on page 33 to learn how.
3. Touch **Edit** in the upper right-hand corner of the screen. The Contact Editing screen appears.
4. Touch **Ringtone**. A list of available ringtones appears.
5. Touch a ringtone. The ringtone plays.
6. Touch **Done**. The ringtone is selected and the Contact Editing screen appears.
7. Touch **Done** at the top of the screen. The ringtone is assigned to the contact.

Note: Refer to "Buying Music and Ringtones in iTunes" *on page 121 to learn how to purchase additional ringtones.*

13. Opening the Photos Application without Closing the Camera

To open the Photos application while the camera is turned on, touch the photo thumbnail in the bottom right-hand corner of the screen.

14. Inserting Emoticons

The Emoji keyboard contains over 460 new emoticons that can be used when entering text. To learn how to add the Emoji keyboard, refer to *"Adding an International Keyboard"* on page 229, and touch **Emoji** in step 6. After adding the Emoji keyboard, touch the ![emoji] key, if the Emoji keyboard is the only one that you have added, or touch the ![globe] key if there are other keyboards in addition to English and Emoji. The Emoji keyboard appears. If you touched the ![globe] key, you may need to touch it again to cycle through the keyboards until the Emoji keyboard turns on.

15. Hiding the Keyboard in the Messages Application

While reading a text message, you can hide the keyboard to view more of the conversation at once. Touch the last visible message in the conversation and slide your finger down to the keyboard. The keyboard is hidden.

16. Controlling Web Surfing Using Gestures

When using the Safari browser, you can touch the ⟨ and ⟩ buttons to go back and forward, respectively. You can also touch the screen and slide your finger to the left or right, respectively, to achieve the same effect.

17. Navigating the Menus Using Gestures

Instead of touching the text in the upper left-hand corner of the screen to return to the previous menu, just touch the left-hand side of the screen and slide your finger to the right. This works in most applications as well, such as the Music application.

18. Pausing or Cancelling an Application Download

When the iPad is downloading more than one application, each application is downloaded one at a time, and in chronological order. For example, if you started to download Angry Birds, and then decided to download Cut the Rope at the same time, Cut the Rope will not download until Angry Birds is installed. If you are downloading more than one application at a time, you may wish to pause one of the downloads so that one of the other applications downloads first. To pause an application download, touch the application icon of the application that you wish to pause. Touch the icon again to resume the download. You may also cancel the download by deleting the application. Refer to *"Deleting an Application"* on page 185 to learn how.

Note: If you cancel a download by deleting the application, you will still be charged if the application was not free. You may still download the application later. Refer to "Buying an Application" *on page 180 to learn how.*

19. Making a Quick Note for a Contact

You may take a quick note for a contact without having to edit the entire contents of the contact. To make a quick note for a contact, touch **Notes** on the contact's information screen. Touch **All Contacts** at the top of the screen to save the note.

20. Using a Search Engine that Does Not Track Your Searches

Safari now allows you to use a new search engine, called DuckDuckGo. This search engine comes from a start-up company, and allows you to search the Web without tracking your searches like Google. Refer to *"Changing the Search Engine"* on page 94 to learn how to change your search engine to DuckDuckGo.

21. Preventing Applications from Refreshing in the Background

Certain applications, such as Podcasts and Weather will refresh their content even when the application is closed. This can drain your battery more quickly. To prevent applications from refreshing in the background:

1. Touch the ![icon] icon. The Settings screen appears.
2. Touch **General**. The General Settings screen appears.
3. Touch **Background App Refresh**. The Background App Refresh screen appears.
4. Touch the ![switch] switch next to 'Background App Refresh'. The ![switch] switch appears and the feature is turned off.

22. Leaving Your Home Screen Free of Icons

If you are a wallpaper connoisseur, you may wish to leave your main Home screen empty. You can move all of your icons to other screens, and leave your main Home screen empty. This way, you can look at your wallpaper all day long without the intrusion of those pesky icons.

23. Call Waiting in FaceTime

FaceTime now allows you to accept another call while you are already on a call. To accept a call and end the current one, touch **End & Accept**. To reject an incoming call, touch **Decline**.

24. Using the Keyboard like a Trackpad

On an iPad, you can control the text cursor on the screen just as you would if you were using a mouse. For example, if you are typing an email, and you want to change the location of the cursor, or select text, use this tip. Touch the keyboard with two fingers, and slide your fingers in any direction. To select text in an email, you still need to touch the first word, and then touch **Select**. However, to select text in an application like Messages or Safari, just drag the two fingers in any direction.

25. Storing Application Folders on the Dock

In addition to application icons, you can store folders on the application dock at the bottom of the screen (the area that remains the same when you navigate to another Home screen). To store a folder on the dock, touch and hold the folder on the Home screen, and drag it to the dock. The dock on the iPad Pro can store up to six items.

26. Using Keyboard Shortcuts on Your Bluetooth Keyboard

When you connect **Apple's Smart Keyboard** to your iPad Pro, you can use keyboard shortcuts to perform tasks more quickly. You can also press and hold the ⌘ key in any application to find out which shortcuts you can use:

⌘ + **Tab**: App switcher

⌘ + **Space**: System-wide search

⌘ + **Shift** + **H**: Navigate to home screen

Shift + **Tab**: Return to the previous field

While Editing Text:

⌘ + **A**: Select all text

⌘ + **X**: Cut

⌘ + **V**: Paste

⌘ + **Z**: Undo

⌘ + **Shift** + **Z**: Redo

Option + **Left**: Move the text cursor one word to the left.

Option + **Right**: Move the text cursor one word to the right.

Option + **Shift** + **Left arrow**: Select the previous word.

Option + **Shift** + **Right arrow**: Select the next word.

Troubleshooting

Table of Contents

1. iPad does not turn on

If the iPad does not power on, try one or more of the following tips:

- **Recharge the iPad** - Use the included wall charger to charge the battery. If the battery power is extremely low, the screen will not turn on for several minutes. Do NOT use the USB port on your computer to charge the iPad.

- **Replace the battery** - If you purchased the iPad a long time ago, you may need to replace the battery. Contact Apple to learn how.

- **Reset the iPad** - This method will not erase any data. Hold down the **Home** button and **Sleep/Wake** button at the same time for 10 seconds. Keep holding the two buttons until the logo appears and the iPad restarts.

2. iPad is not responding

If the iPad is frozen or is not responding, try one or more of the following. These steps solve most problems on the iPad.

- **Exit the application** - If the iPad freezes while running an application, hold the **Home** Button for six seconds. The application quits and the iPad returns to the Home screen.
- **Turn the iPad off and then back on** - If the iPad is still frozen, try pressing the **Sleep/Wake** button to turn the iPad off. Keep holding the **Sleep/Wake** Button until "Slide to Power Off" appears. Slide your finger from left to right over the text. The iPad turns off. After the screen is completely black, press the **Sleep/Wake** button again to turn the iPad back on.
- **Restart the iPad** - Hold the **Home** button and **Sleep/Wake** button at the same time for 10 seconds or until the logo appears.
- **Remove Media** - Some downloaded applications or music may freeze up the iPad. Try deleting some of the media that may be problematic after restarting the iPad. Refer to *"Deleting an Application"* on page 185 to learn how to delete an application. You may also erase all data at once by doing the following:

Warning: Once erased, data cannot be recovered. Make sure you back up any files you wish to keep.

1. Touch the icon. The Settings screen appears.
2. Touch **General**. The General Settings screen appears.
3. Touch **Reset**. The Reset screen appears.
4. Touch **Erase All Content and Settings**. A confirmation dialog appears.
5. Touch **Erase**. Another confirmation dialog appears.
6. Touch **Erase** again. The iPad is erased and reset to factory settings. This process may take several minutes to complete.

3. Can't make a FaceTime call (iPad 4G Only)

If the iPad cannot make outgoing calls, try one of the following:

- If "No Service" is shown at the top of the screen, the network does not cover you in your location. Try moving to a different location, or even to a different part of a building.
- Try walking around to find more signal.
- Turn off Airplane Mode if you have it turned on. If that does not work, try turning Airplane Mode on for 15 seconds and then turning it off. Refer to *"Turning Airplane Mode On or Off"* on page 204 to learn how.
- Make sure you dialed 1 and an area code with the phone number.
- Turn the iPad off and back on.

4. Can't surf the web

If you have no internet access, there may be little or no service in your area. Try moving to a different location or turning Wi-Fi, if available. Refer to *"Using Wi-Fi"* on page 19 to learn how to turn on Wi-Fi. If you still cannot access the Web, refer to *"iPad is not responding"* on page 310 for further assistance.

5. Screen or keyboard does not rotate

If the screen does not rotate, or the full, horizontal keyboard does not appear when you rotate the iPad, it may be one of these issues:

- The application does not support the horizontal view.
- The iPad is lying flat. Hold the iPad upright to change the view in applications that support it.

- The rotation lock is on. The rotation is locked if the ⟳🔒 icon appears next to the battery life at the top of the screen. Touch the bottom of the screen and slide your finger up to access the Control Center. In the control center, touch the ⟳🔒 icon to unlock the rotation.

6. iTunes does not detect iPad when connected to a computer

If iTunes does not detect the iPad when connecting it to your computer, try using a different USB port. If that does not work, turn the iPad off and on again while it is plugged in to the computer. If the iPad indicates that it is connected, the problem might be with your computer. Try restarting your computer or reinstalling iTunes. Otherwise, refer to *"iPad is not responding"* on page 310 for assistance.

7. iPad does not ring or play music, can't hear while talking

Make sure the volume is turned up. Refer to *"Button Layout"* on page 9 to find the Volume Controls. Check whether you can still hear sound through headphones. The headphone jack is located on the top of the iPad. If you can hear sound through headphones, try inserting the headphones and taking them out several times. You may also wish to gently clean the headphone jack, as lint can sometimes make the iPad sounds malfunction. Sometimes the sensor in the headphone jack malfunctions.

8. Low microphone volume, caller can't hear you

If you are talking to someone via FaceTime, and the person cannot hear you, try the following:

- Take off any cases or other accessories as these may cover up the microphone.
- When you first take the iPad out of the box, it comes with a piece of plastic covering the microphone. Make sure to take this plastic off before using the iPad.
- If the caller cannot hear you at all, you may have accidentally muted the conversation.

9. Camera does not work

If the iPad camera is not functioning correctly, try one of the following:

- Clean the camera lens with a polishing cloth.
- Take off any cases or accessories that may interfere with the camera lens on the back of the iPad.
- Hold the iPad steady when taking a picture. A shaky hand often results in a blurry picture. Try leaning against a stationary object to stabilize your hand.
- If you cannot find the icon on your Home screen, try the following:

1. Touch the icon. The Settings screen appears.
2. Touch **General**. The General Settings screen appears.
3. Touch **Restrictions**. The Restrictions screen appears.
4. Touch **Disable Restrictions**. The Restrictions Passcode screen appears.

5. Enter the passcode that you set up when you enabled the restrictions. All restrictions are disabled.

10. iPad shows the White Screen of Death

If the iPad screen has gone completely white, try restarting or restoring the iPad. Refer to *"iPad is not responding"* on page 310 to learn how.

11. "iPad needs to cool down" message appears

If you leave the iPad in your car on a hot day, or expose it to direct sunlight for too long, one of the following may happen:

- iPad stops charging

- Weak signal

- Screen dims

- iPad breaks completely

- "iPad needs to cool down" message appears, where iPad refers to the type of iPad that you have.

Before using the iPad, allow it to cool. The iPad works best in temperatures between 32°F and 95°F (0°C to 35°C). While it is turned off, store the iPad at temperatures between -4°F and 113°F (-20°C to 45°C).

12. Display does not adjust brightness automatically

If the iPad does not brighten in bright conditions, or does not become dimmer in dark conditions, try taking any cases or accessories off. A case may block the light sensor, located at the top of the iPad near the earpiece. Also, check to make sure that Auto-Brightness is turned on. Refer to *"Adjusting the Brightness"* on page 247 to learn how to turn on Auto-Brightness.

Index

Other Books from the Author of the Help Me Series, Charles Hughes

Help Me! Guide to the iPad Air 2

Help Me! Guide to the iPad Air

Help Me! Guide to the Apple Watch

Help Me! Guide to the iPhone 6S

Help Me! Guide to the iPhone 6

Help Me! Guide to the iPhone 5S

Help Me! Guide to iOS 9

Help Me! Guide to the Nexus 7

Help Me! Guide to the Galaxy S5

Help Me! Guide to the Kindle Fire HDX

Help Me! Guide to the HTC One

Help Me! Guide to the iPhone 4

Help Me! Guide to the iPod Touch

Help Me! Guide to the iPad Mini

Help Me! Guide to the Kindle Touch

Help Me! Guide to the Samsumg Galaxy Note

42739091R00178

Made in the USA
Middletown, DE
20 April 2017